The Road to Emmaus

The Road to Emmaus

PILGRIMAGE as a WAY of LIFE

Jim Forest

ORBIS BOOKS

Maryknoll, New York 10545

Founded in 1970, Orbis Books endeavors to publish works that enlighten the mind, nourish the spirit, and challenge the conscience. The publishing arm of the Maryknoll Fathers and Brothers, Orbis seeks to explore the global dimensions of the Christian faith and mission, to invite dialogue with diverse cultures and religious traditions, and to serve the cause of reconciliation and peace. The books published reflect the views of their authors and do not represent the official position of the Maryknoll Society. To learn more about Maryknoll and Orbis Books, please visit our website at www.maryknoll.org.

Manufactured in the United States of America.
Manuscript editing and typesetting by Joan Weber Laflamme.

Cataloguing-in-Publication Data

Forest, Jim.
   The road to Emmaus : pilgrimage as a way of life / Jim Forest.
    p. cm.
   Includes bibliographical references.
   ISBN 978-1-57075-731-0
  1. Christian pilgrims and pilgrimages. 2. Spiritual life–Catholic Church. I. Title.
   BX2323.F67 2007
   263'.041–dc22

                        2007005778

A pilgrim is anyone who is out of his own country.
　　　　　　　　　　　　　—DANTE, *LA VITA NUOVA*

The search is what anyone would undertake if he were not sunk in the everydayness of his own life. . . . To become aware of the possibility of the search is to be on to something. Not to be on to something is to be in despair.
　　　　　　　　　　—WALKER PERCY, *THE MOVIEGOER*

All joy, as distinct from mere pleasure, still more amusement, emphasizes our pilgrim status; always reminds, beckons, awakens desire. Our best havings are wantings.
　　　—C. S. LEWIS, LETTER DATED NOVEMBER 5, 1959

The geographical pilgrimage is the symbolic acting out of an inner journey. The inner journey is the interpolation of the meanings and signs of the outer journey. One can have one without the other. It is better to have both.
　　　　　—THOMAS MERTON, *MYSTICS AND ZEN MASTERS*

With gratitude to several fellow pilgrims:

My wife, Nancy
Tom and Monica Cornell
Robert and Peggy Ellsberg
Ivan Sewter
Harry and Lyn Isbell
Fr. Sergei and Aliona Ovsiannikov

Contents

Pilgrims, Canterbury Tales

Introduction

Pilgrim. For a child growing up in America, the word *Pilgrim* had no religious connotations. Mainly heard in the plural, Pilgrims referred to a community of storm-defying, black-clad English Puritans who crossed the Atlantic on the *Mayflower,* founding the village of Plymouth on the edge of Massachusetts Bay in December 1620. It wasn't the destination the Pilgrims intended–their goal had been Virginia–but where a furious winter storm delivered them. Pilgrims that they were, they accepted this as God's will. The following fall the Pilgrims, with the local Indians who had helped them survive, organized a feast to celebrate a successful harvest. It was the origin of America's favorite annual holiday. The feast of Thanksgiving turned *Pilgrim* into a word a child could inhale, two syllables that smelled of stuffed turkey, cranberry sauce, sweet potatoes, creamed onions, and pumpkin pie.

It was in eighth grade that I discovered that, long before the *Mayflower* set sail, there was another sort of pilgrim. This news came from the *World Book Encyclopedia,* a handsomely bound set of books a meter wide that some generous soul had donated to the school and that providentially had landed in my classroom. It seemed to me a gift that had fallen out of heaven. I read my way through it, beginning with the first volume on the left: *Aardvark to Bermuda.* In the second volume I discovered an illustration from an early copy of Chaucer's *Canterbury Tales,* a medieval picture of a group of colorfully dressed men and women making their way on horseback from London to Canterbury Cathedral under a lapis lazuli sky. Inside the cathedral, the text explained, Archbishop Thomas Becket had been murdered by knights of King Henry II on December 29, 1170, the churchman's skull split by a sword. In the same instant Thomas Becket was made a holy martyr—and bloodstained Canterbury turned into a magnet for anyone drawn to pilgrimage.

Perhaps it was here that I was first confronted with a language both familiar and foreign, Middle English:

> *Whan that aprill with his shoures soote*
> *The droghte of march hath perced to the roote,*
> *And bathed every veyne in swich licour*
> *Of which vertu engendred is the flour;*
> *Whan zephirus eek with his sweete breeth*
> *Inspired hath in every holt and heeth*
> *Tendre croppes, and the yonge sonne*
> *Hath in the ram his halve cours yronne,*
> *And smale foweles maken melodye,*
> *That slepen al the nyght with open ye*
> *(so priketh hem nature in hir corages);*
> *Thanne longen folk to goon on pilgrimages*
> *And palmeres for to seken straunge strondes,*
> *To ferne halwes, kowthe in sondry londes;*
> *And specially from every shires ende*
> *Of engelond to caunterbury they wende,*
> *The hooly blisful martir for to seke,*
> *That hem hath holpen whan that they were seeke.*

"Aprill with his shoures soote?" While Aprill has only dropped its final *L* on its way to modern English, it takes a minute to connect *shoures* with *showers* and *soote* with *sweet.* "Logen folk to goon on pilgrimages?" People long to go on pilgrimages . . . not so hard. "Hooly blisful martir?" Holy, blissful martyr—an easy phrase.

Is it possible that my first encounter with Middle English came that early? This was New Jersey in the 1950s. It would have been daring for the World Book, a product as American as a box of Cheerios, to test its young readers with so many unfamiliar spellings and long-abandoned verb forms. But at least there was that eye-widening picture of colorful men and women on pony-sized horses setting off under a sky as blue as a robin's egg, and a text at least mentioning Chaucer, the fourteenth-century English poet whose unhurried pilgrims traded tales, creating a pathway of stories linking London to Canterbury.

Pilgrimage. Almost the same as *pilgrim,* yet the added syllable created another word to ponder. It made my thoughts leap across the Atlantic to the Old World of medieval days. The idea of riding on a horse while sharing tales with fellow travelers made pilgrimage seem an appealing adventure. While I knew very little about bishops and kings, and still less about King Henry's motives in wanting an archbishop's life cut short by the sword, it wasn't necessary for anyone to explain to a thirteen-year-old boy why the bloodstained floor of a church might become a spot to which people would be powerfully drawn.

My first full-scale pilgrimage book was *Huckleberry Finn,* Mark Twain's tale of a runaway boy and escaped slave traveling at night by raft down the Mississippi River. There were no holy martyr's bones pulling them forward, just the river's insistent flow, but these two travelers were on a kind of pilgrimage: a search for freedom. Floating on the nighttime currents of the Mississippi River, staring upward at diamond-bright stars, struck me as a much better way to begin a dialogue with the universe than in a classroom. Not that Mark Twain called their quest a pilgrimage. His book made no reference to Huck and Jim being on any sort of religious pursuit. Yet I sensed that their journey, for all its hazards and despite the absence of shrines or relics, offered these two travelers occasional glimpses of heaven.

If I had been in school half a century earlier, John Bunyan's *The Pilgrim's Progress* would surely have been assigned reading. In the English-speaking world from the late seventeenth century until well into the twentieth, it was a book nearly as popular as the Bible. Indeed, many homes had those two books and no others. But by the 1950s, I wonder if there was a single copy of Bunyan's book in our school library? If there was, I never spotted it.

It wasn't until I was taking a survey course in English Literature at Hunter College in Manhattan that I read John Bunyan's book. The central figure, Christian, is an everyman character trying to find his way from the City of Destruction to the Celestial City. It is no easy journey. The obstacles are many. He is directed to find the Wicket Gate, representing the entrance to the "narrow way" that Christ speaks of in the gospel, but he is led astray by Mr. Worldly Wiseman as well as Mr. Legality and his son Civility, inhabitants of the village of Morality. Yet at last Christian finds the Wicket Gate, where he is granted a vision of Jesus himself.

Bunyon's book helped me understand that the word *pilgrim* could be used in a metaphorical sense: every life without exception a nonstop pilgrimage from the womb to the grave, a successful pilgrimage if one made it to heaven, a tragic failure if one fell into hell.

It was at Hunter College that I finally read *The Canterbury Tales,* struggling with Middle English but also enchanted by it. I was amazed to discover that people on pilgrimage were not necessarily talking about "holy things." One of the pilgrims told of a student lodger seducing his landlord's wife while convincing her dimwitted husband to hide in a barrel as the world was within hours of its final doom. There was more bawdy humor and sexual candor in Chaucer's pilgrims than I had yet come upon in modern literature.

I came to Hunter College as a part-time student in the fall of 1961, having a few months earlier been given an early discharge from the Navy on grounds of conscientious objection. Except for one night a week studying English literature, my time was chiefly spent with the Catholic Worker community on Chrystie Street in lower Manhattan, a place that gave yet another meaning to the word *pilgrimage.*

The founder of the community, and its dominating presence, was Dorothy Day. Her column in the monthly newspaper we published, *The Catholic Worker,* was called "On Pilgrimage." This was an ongoing diary—news of Dorothy's travels but also accounts of visitors, books she was reading, talks she had attended, perhaps even the opera she had heard by radio the previous Sunday afternoon. Dorothy gave the word *pilgrimage* a meaning that was immediate rather than medieval. It was along John Bunyan lines: every day of one's life and all that happened along the way, planned or unexpected, were segments of a heavenward pilgrimage, so long as the guiding principle was to live the gospel and to discover Christ in those whom one encountered. Pilgrimage for Dorothy was a way of life, a mode of listening, an attitude that motivated choices, a discipline of being.

I began to regard my own life in terms of pilgrimage.

There were many small pilgrimages to churches in Manhattan, walking to some, taking the subway to others. In those days one could assume any Catholic church would be open throughout the day and even through the night. Thus at the end of every journey was a place to pray in the presence of the Blessed Sacrament.

There were also pilgrim outings to some of the world's best museums: the Metropolitan, the Cloisters, the Museum of Modern Art, the Pierpont Morgan Library. To visit them as an act of pilgrimage was somehow different from seeing art as a tourist with a little time on his hands.

A more challenging experiment in pilgrimage was a late summer bicycle ride from lower Manhattan to St. Joseph's Abbey, a Trappist monastery near Spencer in western Massachusetts. Traveling with less than twenty dollars in my pocket, I slept in orchards along the way. Luckily, the weather was hospitable. So were the monks. To make myself more presentable, I had first gone to a barber shop in the nearby town and gotten my first (and last) professional shave, a major but useful investment. Though I was entirely unexpected and probably the only guest in a long time to reach their monastery by bicycle, I was given use of a bed in the guesthouse attic, a job helping in the guest-house kitchen, and was invited to attend talks being given by one of the monks to retreatants, mainly monsignors who had arrived on four wheels rather than two.

The next major pilgrimage came in the winter, this time hitchhiking, starting from Spring Street in lower Manhattan with the Trappist Abbey of Gethsemani in Kentucky as my destination—a thousand miles of petitionary travel in weather that was not only cold but often wet and icy. I remember standing long, dark hours in sleet outside a truck stop in Pennsylvania waiting for a driver to pull over and offer a lift. Many plastic statues of Jesus and Mary sailed by in rain-spattered cars and trucks. Two and a half days later, in the late afternoon, my fellow hitchhiker Bob Kaye and I stood at the monastery gate, exhausted but happy as children on Christmas morning. This time I was expected. The visit had begun with an invitation from one of the monks, the writer Thomas Merton, but our date of arrival was approximate, as was the length of our stay. This time I had failed to see a barber first. The abbot, Dom James, quickly passed the word through Merton that if this particular shaggy pilgrim was to stay more than one night, he must have a haircut. This occurred the next morning in a basement room where monastic haircuts were dispensed that put the recipient in a state of near baldness. Though in principal Trappist monks aim for silence, and in those days did most of their communicating by sign language, the novices stood around me in a state of continuous laughter as my hair fell to the concrete floor. Merton told me I looked like a young Gandhi. All I needed was a loincloth and walking stick.

There have been many pilgrimages since then, some on foot, some by bike, others by car and train and even airplane.

The jewel of them all was a three-month stay between Jerusalem and Bethlehem in the spring of 1985. After all, for the Christian, Jerusalem—as the city of Christ's resurrection—will always be the center of the world. Bethlehem, the town of his birth, is nearby, less than a day's walk. In the course of twenty centuries, millions of Christians have made the Holy Land their goal, with Jerusalem being the most important single place to walk and pray, and Bethlehem a close second.

That spring I was teaching at the Ecumenical Institute, a graduate school with links to the University of Notre Dame. As we had children to care for, one still in diapers, Nancy and I generally took turns going into Jerusalem or Bethlehem for days of pilgrimage. While one was being a pilgrim, the other stayed at Tantur taking care of the kids.

It was in the course of one of these frequent visits to Jerusalem, while standing in line to enter the tomb where Christ's body was laid after his crucifixion and in which he rose from the dead, that Nancy found herself standing behind a married couple. Behind her was a group of Greek women in black, each woman holding as many candles as her hands could grasp. The man and woman in front of her were trying to decide where they were.

"Is this where he was born?" the wife asked. "No," her husband answered, "that was yesterday—Bethlehem." They went inside the small tomb, took photos, and left, still unclear where they had been. All the while the Greek women were quietly weeping. When it was their turn, one by one they knelt by the stone slab that for them marked the center of the cosmos, the exact spot where Christ, God incarnate, had risen from death. They lit their candles and then, leaving the tomb, blew them out. Now they had a precious gift for relatives and friends at home: candles that had been burned in the place of the resurrection.

"Today I stood on the borderline between tourism and pilgrimage," Nancy told me that evening.

Most of us are a mixture of tourist and pilgrim.

In the spring of 1941, not many months before he became a monk, Thomas Merton went on pilgrimage to southeastern Cuba with the goal of visiting Cobré, a shrine to the Virgin Mary, but he spent days in Havana as well. He looked back on his visit as "ninety percent tourism, ten percent pilgrimage."

Perhaps this is as much pilgrimage as most of us can stand. We are like Chaucer's travelers to Canterbury, spending more time with mugs of beer in our hands than rosaries. But even to be ten percent pilgrim is no small achievement.

According to Saint Paul, being a pilgrim is the calling of every Christian. We become strangers and pilgrims the moment we realize we are seeking the kingdom of God. As he put it in his Letter to the Hebrews:

> All of these [our spiritual ancestors, beginning with Abraham and Sarah, Isaac and Jacob] died in faith without having received the promises, but from a distance they saw and greeted them. They confessed that they were strangers and foreigners on the earth, for people who speak in this way make it clear that they are seeking a homeland. If they had been thinking of the land that they had left behind, they would have had opportunity to return. But as it is, they desire a better country, that is, a heavenly one. Therefore God is not ashamed to be called their God; indeed, he has prepared a city for them. (Hebrews 11:13–16)

This book attempts to look at what it means to be a pilgrim—both as a way of living ordinary life, no matter where you happen to be, and also in the more limited sense of traveling toward one of God's "thin places," as places that draw pilgrims tend to be. No matter how short the distances and familiar the route you travel on a given day, you can do it as a pilgrim—and no matter how long the journey or how sacred its destination, it is possible to be nothing more than a tourist. Whether the journey is within your own backyard or takes you to the other side of the world, the potential is there for the greatest of adventures: a journey not only toward Christ but with him.

The Road

Consider well the highway, the road by which you went.
—JEREMIAH 31:21

[The road] was the most imperative and first of our necessities. It is older than buildings and than wells.
—HILLAIRE BELLOC, *THE OLD ROAD*

Now my body seemed to walk itself, the road walking my body.
—AN AMERICAN PILGRIM RECALLING HIS JOURNEY
TO SANTIAGO DE COMPOSTELA

One could spend long hours making a list of great human achievements—from the wheel to the great cathedrals to the discovery of DNA and the development of computers—and yet leave out one of the most important attainments because it is too obvious, too ordinary, and too ancient: the road. Roads are the circulatory system of the human race and the original information highway. From times long before the written word, roads have linked house to house, town to town, and city to city. Without roads there are no communities. Roads not only connect towns but give birth to them. They pass through all borders, checkpoints, and barriers, connecting not only friend to friend but foe to foe. Far older than passports, the road is an invitation to cross frontiers, to start a dialogue, to end enmity. Each road gives witness to the need we have to be in touch with one another.

1

There was a time before roads when the world was pure wilderness, but even before Adam and Eve there would have been countless tracks and paths created by animals that moved in packs or herds, following their prey or migrating with the seasons. With the arrival of human beings, many of these pathways would have become roads for hunters, here and there providing ideal sites for encampments and villages.

Supreme collective endeavor that they are, roads reveal the cultures that made them. Roman roads tend to run straight as Roman laws, but in many cultures roads take many turns as they search out fords, avoid marshes, find higher ground, touch wells and pubs, and seek holy places.

Roads are life giving. They provide the primary infrastructure of social life. Without them, there is no commerce. Without roads and the delivery systems they support, we would starve. Even more important than safeguarding weights and measures and punishing those who watered down the beer, it was the primary task of kings and queens to maintain and keep safe the highways.

Human history is the history of roads. Empires have been ranked according to the quality of their highways. Roman highways were so well built that even today, two millennia later, portions of them not only survive but remain in use.

Roads mark the way to safety. Paths tells the traveler how to get round a chasm or find a ford to cross the river. They point the way through marshes and around quicksand.

If roads sometimes speed armies on the path of destruction, more often they guide pilgrims toward encounters with the sacred. They connect not only capital cities and great cathedrals but remote churches that house the relics of saints. A saint's relics have many times widened a road or even created a new one.

Roads not only take us toward each other but, when we need to be rescued from society, they lead us to solitude.

The same road that leads to Rome is, in reverse and at its furthest reaches, a route to the desert.

Roads have a sacramental aspect: a road is a visible sign of a hidden unity. Roads are a map of human connectedness.

The road is a primary metaphor. In the gospel Christ speaks of choosing the narrow path rather than the broad highway. Early Christians called themselves followers of the Way.

The road has often been a place of religious breakthroughs. Two disciples walked with the risen Christ on the road to Emmaus, unaware of who he was. Later they took the same road back to Jerusalem, where they related how Christ had revealed himself to them in the breaking of the bread.

Paul–Christianity's first great pilgrim–encountered Christ on the road to Damascus. Traversing the highways of the Roman Empire, Paul became one of history's great men of the road.

Old roads still exist. In some cases they are quite visible and still in use; in some they are hidden under modern highways; in still other cases they are grassy pathways once again; and in some places they are hardly more than faint indentations in the soil.

The old pilgrim road from Winchester to Canterbury is in turn all of these. A road as old as England, some parts are now rarely walked, while other sections have become major motorways. Yet, in part thanks to a steady trickle of pilgrims still making their way to the church where Saint Thomas Becket was murdered in 1170, the pilgrim path still exists from end to end. In 1904 Hillaire Belloc published *The Old Road*,[1] in which he managed to stitch together the road's fragments into a continuous whole, which he himself walked in one of his many acts of pilgrimage.

One of the pilgrims of recent years, Shirley du Boulay, walked from Winchester to Canterbury in the early 1990s and has left us one of the best contemporary memoirs of pilgrimage, *The Road to Canterbury*. Old roads, she writes,

> are hallowed by time and the footsteps of men and animals. . . . We respond to old roads as to old buildings. Even their names—Watling Street, Ermine Street, the Fosse Way, the Maiden Way, Stane Street—echo in the imagination. I remember as a child being told, as we walked the Berkshire Downs, that we were on a Roman Road called Icknield Street. I remember too my pride thereafter in recognizing a long straight road as Roman. . . . A road does not just appear. It is the fruit of long years of trial and error. It is the supreme collective endeavor, a long experiment in which the individual can only be subsumed.[2]

It's a special feeling walking an old road. The pilgrim may see no one else behind or ahead and yet be profoundly aware of not being alone. Hundreds of thousands of others have passed this way, generation after generation. At times the multi-generational river of travelers seems almost visible. If a file of medieval pilgrims were to appear before us on small horses, Chaucer himself among them, it would hardly be surprising.

Among those who walked or rode before us, not all were pilgrims heading toward a shrine, but many were, and even those on more prosaic errands may have traveled with the God-alert attitude of a pilgrim. Many were people aware that each step they took was an act of prayer. Roads that have been intensively used by people at prayer seem afterward to hold a rumor of prayer. The road itself becomes a thin place.

One of the celebrators of the road was the Oxford don J. R. R. Tolkien, through whom an invented history of Middle Earth made its way into the modern world. Both *The Hobbit* and *The Lord of the Rings* are a celebration of roads. For Tolkien, it wasn't *roads* in the plural but simply *the Road,* singular. However many intersections, however many forks along the way, however many rarely walked paths reach out from it, all the tracks human beings walk are connected and form a single system, like the body's capillary system, through which a single river of blood makes its way away from the heart to the remotest cell and back again.

Tolkien's Bilbo sang the song of the road as he took his first step along a path that led at last to the edge of death in his encounter with a dragon. Bilbo's heir, Frodo, sang it as he stepped out the door of his snug burrow on his way to overthrow a kingdom of evil, though at the time all he was aware of was his hope of delivering a magic ring to a place of safety: Rivendell.

The core text of Tolkien's tales is Bilbo and Frodo's song, which celebrates stepping out the door into the unknown without the certainty that one will ever see one's home again:

> *The Road goes ever on and on*
> *Down from the door where it began.*
> *Now far ahead the Road has gone,*
> *And I must follow, if I can,*
> *Pursuing it with eager feet,*
> *Until it joins some larger way*
> *Where many paths and errands meet.*
> *And whither then? I cannot say.*[3]

Walking

If we live by the Spirit, let us also walk by the Spirit.

—SAINT PAUL, GALATIANS 5:25

If you would attain to what you are not yet, you must always be displeased by what you are. For where you are pleased with yourself there you have remained. Keep adding, keep walking, keep advancing.

—SAINT AUGUSTINE

It is no use walking anywhere to preach unless our walking is our preaching.

—SAINT FRANCIS OF ASSISI

The fundamental action of a human being is walking upright.

—BENEDICTA WARD, *TO BE A PILGRIM*

We live in a world in which body and soul are often seen as innately at odds with each other. For those who think along those lines, death is regarded as a freeing of the soul from its long imprisonment in the flesh—the canary of the spirit released from its rusting cage. This concept is rooted in Gnosticism. For those seeking to adapt Christ and his gospel to the anti-material dimension of Gnostic theology, the portrait of Jesus provided by the gospels is completely wrong. There was no virgin birth—neither a virgin nor a birth was required, nor crucifixion and death on the cross, as Jesus was in reality pure spirit, only appearing to be a human being. There was no resurrection, because he never died.

In contrast, orthodox Christian teaching permanently connects body and soul. The Second Person of the Holy Trinity became human in the womb of Mary, was born as any child is born, grew as any child grows, bled as does anyone who is wounded. The bare feet of Christ we see in icons touched the earth just as solidly as our feet do. When he abandoned the tomb, he still had a physical body.

Each of us is simultaneously a physical and a spiritual being. Having a spiritual life does not mean repressing or shedding a physical life. It's not one or the other. Only angels are spiritual creatures. Not us. In an event prefigured by Christ's resurrection, we too will rise from death, body and soul.

Meanwhile, nothing we do is meant to be "merely" physical or "purely" spiritual. Every act has the potential of uniting the physical and the spiritual—not only receiving communion or making the sign of the cross or kissing an icon, but also shopping, house cleaning, playing a game, washing the dishes, or making love. Even our most intangible thoughts and daydreams occur mysteriously in our tangible flesh.

Walking is one of life's simple things. No special talent is required. All one needs is a pair of functional legs and the will to put one foot in front of the other. Walking is a physical activity that is meant to have spiritual significance.

Few human activities are more basic than walking, and few more taken for granted. We need only watch an infant to be reminded that walking is a hard-won achievement. Learning to walk is one of the main projects of our first year of life. Somehow it dawns on us at a very early age that getting around on two legs might be better than crawling—at the very least, it frees up our hands for other uses. Then begins the campaign to stand, and then—harder yet—to move while standing. Once this miracle is achieved and the pa-

rental applause dies down, it is something we do daily, minus ovations, until accident or illness or old age stops us, at which point we struggle to finds ways either to regain the use of our legs and walk again or to find some other way to get around. (My Aunt Douglas, when she celebrated her ninetieth birthday, was annoyed with those in the family who suggested that, as she could no longer easily see over the steering wheel, it was time to give up driving. It was her intention, she said with determination, "to drive all the way to the cemetery." Luckily for those endangered by her driving, at last she changed her mind and retired from the role of driver.)

No one takes kindly to being restricted to a small space. Few things are more hateful than being immobilized. To live within a small enclosure is for most of us an experience that approximates hell. One of the worst aspects of being imprisoned is that movement is drastically curtailed. Nor is ordinary imprisonment as bad as it gets. Just as a Russian *matrioshka* doll contains dolls within dolls, prisons contain prisons. When a prisoner is punished, the penalty is an even greater restriction of space and mobility—being placed in solitary confinement. Yet even within the smallest cell, a prisoner will spend part of the day walking, all the while longing for the freedom to move once again in the open air.

Unimpeded walking is one of life's most ordinary, least expensive, and deeply rewarding pleasures. With little effort, putting one foot in front of the other and going forward can provide a foretaste of heaven.

One of the people I learned this from was Dorothy Day. She saw every journey, even the most local, in terms of pilgrimage. Though living in a derelict part of Manhattan that most New Yorkers took pains to avoid, Dorothy had an endless ability to discover beauty in unlikely places. She rejoiced at the sight of grass breaking through cracks in the pavement, was exultant at the smell of garlic escaping a kitchen, and gazed joyfully at flowers blooming in a tenement window.

One of the early turning points in Dorothy's life was linked with walks she took on the west side of Chicago when she was in her early teens. The inspiration to do so came from reading Upton Sinclair's novel *The Jungle*. The west side was an area packed with immigrants, stock yards and meat-processing plants. She walked for miles, pushing her baby brother in his carriage, while exploring "interminable grey streets, fascinating in their dreary sameness, past tavern after tavern."

She found beauty in the midst of desolation:

There were tiny flower gardens and vegetable patches in the yards. Often there were rows of corn, stunted but still recognizable, a few tomato plants, and always the vegetables were bordered by flowers, often grateful marigolds, all sizes and shades with their pungent odor. The odor of geranium leaves, tomato plants, marigolds; the smell of lumber, of tar, of roasting coffee; the smell of good bread and rolls and coffee cake coming from the small German bakeries. Here was enough beauty to satisfy me.[4]

Her long walks in the slums were truly eye-opening experiences. She could no longer look on the poor as shiftless, worthless people whose sufferings were no one's fault but their own. Walking such streets as a fifteen year old, she pondered the poor and the workers and felt "that from then on my life was to be linked to theirs, their interests were to be mine: I had received a call, a vocation, a direction in my life."[5]

It must have been partly thanks to Dorothy that I gradually found a similar capacity to notice beauty even in places of chronic ugliness. I still recall the rapture I experienced while spending a year in a high-walled prison when, walking from my cell block to the dining hall, I saw the reflection of the sunrise on windows just high enough to mirror the light: the windows streaked with molten gold and raspberry light. It was breathtaking.[6]

"Everywhere is in walking distance, if you have the time," comments comedian Stephen Wright. It's true. If you give yourself the time and freedom, and allowing sea or air passage of any oceans in the way, you can walk to Santiago de Compostela or even to Jerusalem. But if such major stretches are out of reach because of other commitments, you can be on pilgrimage in your own small patch of the world.

Part of the work of a pilgrim is to be surprised. As G. K. Chesterton wrote, "I am astonished at the people who are not astonished." While being in unfamiliar places may make it easier to be surprised, you can be surprised right where you are. No matter how many times you have walked around the same block, there is always something or someone new to see, some detail previously not noticed. To pay attention to passing faces is a school of meditation and prayer.

Walking can be a school of wordless theology. Many see Christianity as both complex and cerebral, entered by means of theological studies that can be mastered only by the very clever and highly literate after long years of study. As Benedicta Ward writes:

> It is possible also to come at Christianity from a rather different point of view as well, seeing it as something not too difficult but too simple for us, too basic, something to be apprehended therefore through the most simple thing that we all have, our bodies, by walking, by kneeling and bowing, by standing still. . . . The object of the subtleties of the theologians . . . must be as accessible to the least intellectually alert as to the most complex mind, to a child as much as to a scholar.[7]

It was from a Vietnamese Buddhist monk, Thich Nhat Hanh, that I first became aware of walking as an opportunity to repair the damaged connection between the physical and the spiritual. In the late 1960s he asked me to accompany him on his lecture trips in the United States. He spoke to audiences about Vietnamese culture and what the war looked like to ordinary Vietnamese people. At times he also spoke about the monastic vocation and meditation.

In conversation, Nhat Hanh sometimes spoke of the importance of what he called "mindful breathing," a phrase that seemed quite odd to me at first. Yet I was aware that his walking was somehow different from mine and could imagine this might have something to do with his way of breathing. Even if we were late for an appointment, he walked in an attentive, unhurried way.

It wasn't until we climbed the steps to my sixth-floor apartment in Manhattan that I began to take his example to heart. Though in my late twenties and very fit, I was out of breath by the time I reached my front door. Nhat Hanh, on the other hand, seemed rested. I asked him how he did that. "You have to learn how to breathe while you walk," he replied. "Let's go back to the bottom and walk up again. I will show you how to breathe while climbing stairs." On the way back up, he quietly described how he was breathing. It wasn't a difficult lesson. Linking slow, attentive breaths with taking the stairs made an astonishing difference. The climb took one or two minutes longer, but when I reached my door I found myself refreshed instead of depleted.

In the 1970s I spent time in France with Nhat Hanh on a yearly basis. He was better known then—his home had become for many people a center of pilgrimage. One of the things I found him teaching was his method of attentive walking. Once a day all his guests would set off in a silent procession led by him. The walk was prefaced with his advice that we practice slow, mindful breathing while at the same time being aware of each footstep, seeing each moment of contact between foot and earth as a prayer for peace. We went single file, moving slowly, deeply aware of the texture of the earth and grass, the scent of the air, the movement of leaves in the trees, the sound of insects and birds. Many times as I walked I was reminded of the words of

Jesus: "You must be like little children to enter the kingdom of heaven." Such attentive walking was a return to the hyper-alertness of childhood.

Mindful breathing connected with mindful walking gradually becomes normal. It is then a small step to connect walking and breathing with prayer.

Long-distance hiking shoes are not needed. Even walking to a nearby shop that you have been to countless times can be a small pilgrimage—noticing the particular light of that moment in time, inhaling the smell of the day, getting a glimpse of life in other houses, pausing to admire how a building has suddenly been gilded by the late-afternoon light. "Been there, done that" is definitely not a pilgrim attitude. Boredom is a graveyard symptom.

You can walk to some great shrine on a journey that takes weeks or months and fail to become a pilgrim. Walking a pilgrimage route, wearing a pilgrim's badge, and sleeping in pilgrim hostels are not what make a pilgrim. Pilgrimage is more an attitude than an act. If all you are seeking is exercise, diversion, or a deed that will slim your body or impress your friends, you might be happier racking up miles on an exercise cycle at the local gym. Pilgrimage is a conscious act of seeking a more vital awareness of God's living presence. As was said in medieval times, "If you do not travel with the King whom you seek, you will not find him at the end of your journey."

One need not walk to pray, but most of us do at least some walking and can use those spaces to make a beginning with prayer. Were we to discover the opportunity for prayer that walking provides, we might find ourselves doing a great deal more walking. Walking and praying, no matter what the destination, we may find we have become pilgrims along the way.

Praying

Then Jesus told them a parable about their need to pray always and not to lose heart.

—LUKE 18:1

To pray is to pay attention to something or someone other than oneself. Whenever a man so concentrates his attention—on a landscape, a poem, a geometrical problem, an idol, or the True God—that he completely forgets his own ego and desires, he is praying.

—W. H. AUDEN

Prayer is first of all listening to God. It's openness. God is always speaking, always doing something. Prayer is to enter into that activity. . . . Convert your thoughts into prayer. As we are involved in unceasing thinking, so we are called to unceasing prayer. The difference is not that prayer is thinking about other things, but that prayer is thinking in dialogue . . . a conversation with God.

—HENRI NOUWEN

Prayer is an act of intimacy between created being and Creator. It can happen while among a crowd of people in church or occur in solitude. It can happen in the blink of an eye or fill an entire day.

There are many forms of prayer and schools of prayer, but in every case prayer seeks contact with God. "Christian prayer is the simple act of addressing God as 'you,'" the Benedictine monk Abbot Christopher Jamison has written.[8] "Prayer is descending with the mind into your heart," wrote the great Russian teacher of prayer Saint Theofan the Recluse, "and there standing before the face of the Lord, ever present, all seeing, within you. . . . It is only when our hearts appeal to God that our reading prayers becomes a true prayer, otherwise it is not yet a prayer."[9]

Prayer is anything we do to be aware of God's presence. It is a state of being in which we become awake to God's closeness. This God-awareness can be so intense that time seems to stop and distances disappear, yet one can pray even while being aware of every distraction: the buzz of a fly, the noise of traffic, the ticking of a clock.

Silence can be a prayer. One can pray simply by attentive listening to God. Just to be in a state of active listening becomes an act of communion with creation as it is continuously renewed by God's being. This silence is far from silent.

Many rely on prayer aids like the Catholic rosary or the Orthodox prayer rope, in which silence and word touch each other seamlessly. For Catholics, the main prayer used is the Hail Mary; for Orthodox Christians, it is the Jesus Prayer (also called the Prayer of the Heart).

Some people have a gift to pray in a conversational way with God; it is not that they hear God's response in words, but they sense their words are being heard. However don't be alarmed if this sort of prayer isn't your gift. I am not one for making up prayers on the spur of the moment. When I try, they often seem painfully inadequate, forced, and too self-conscious.

Most of the time I rely on traditional prayers in widespread Christian usage. I like to recite prayers handed down from earlier centuries, prayers polished by generations of use and available to those who care to make them their own.

Once such a traditional prayer has been learned by heart, it is available no matter where you are or what you are doing. As you memorize more prayers and psalms, the richer your prayer life becomes, but even one prayer, recited over and over, can be enough. The prayer isn't your own composition, yet it becomes your own.

A good posture for prayer is standing. Not only does it help keep you alert, but it is body language for the resurrection.

Make the sign of the cross at appropriate moments while praying, for example, whenever saying the words "Father, Son, and Holy Spirit." Such a gesture links body and soul.

If you have an icon corner, pray there at least once or twice a day. (An icon corner doesn't have to be in a corner. It might be a shelf with a few icons and a candle or vigil lamp.[10])

When you wash dishes, try using the time for prayer. I once was advised by my Buddhist friend Thich Nhat Hanh to "wash every dish as if it were the baby Jesus."

Praying goes well with walking, no matter how short or long the path. In my own case, I often do my morning prayers while walking in a nearby park. As walking is something nearly all of us do every day, praying while walking is simply making better use of time spent on your feet.

Among those in whom walking and praying are forever linked is the author of *The Way of the Pilgrim,* a book that has become a classic in many languages. The nineteenth-century author's name is unknown, but through his work many people have been introduced to the Jesus Prayer.

The beginning of *The Way of the Pilgrim* could hardly be simpler:

By the grace of God I am a Christian man, by my actions a great sinner, and by my calling a homeless wanderer of the humblest birth who roams from place to place. My worldly goods are a knapsack with some dried bread in it on my back, and in my breast pocket a Bible. And that is all.[11]

One Sunday, attending the liturgy, the pilgrim happens to hear the section of Saint Paul's Letter to the Thessalonians that summons Christ's followers to pray without ceasing, at all times, and in all places. He begins to wonder if uninterrupted prayer is actually possible. After all, there are many concerns in life that cry out for attention and seem to edge out prayer. Is it likely that Saint Paul meant his words to be taken literally?

The question haunts him to such an extent that he sets off to a succession of churches, near and far, to hear what respected priests have to say on the topic. At each place he visits he hears helpful words about prayer—what it is, how much we need it, the good fruit it bears—yet no one seems able to explain how constant prayer is to be achieved, prayer that would even be part of one's sleep. No one seems to think that Saint Paul's phrase about "ceaseless prayer" is to be taken literally. Finally, the narrator decides the only thing to be done is to seek out "an experienced and skilled person who would give me in conversation that teaching about unceasing prayer which drew me so urgently."

Pilgrim that he is, with no need of a job and no deadlines to meet, he is more than willing to walk to the ends of the earth in his search for a teacher.

After a year of walking, one evening the pilgrim encounters an elderly monk making his way to a nearby monastery. Once again the pilgrim asks his burning question. The monk responds with enthusiasm: "Thank God, my dear brother, for having revealed to you this unappeasable desire for unceasing interior prayer. Recognize in it the call of God and calm yourself." Walking side by side, they make their way to the monastery.

At the heart of the pilgrim's search, the monk points out as they walk, are the questions: "What is prayer? And how does one learn to pray?"

The elder stresses the primacy of prayer in daily life: "Many people reason quite the wrong way about prayer, imagining that good actions and all sorts of preliminary measures render us capable of prayer. But quite the reverse is the case. It is prayer which bears fruit in good works. . . . Prayer is the mother of all spiritual blessings. . . . Learn first to acquire the spirit of prayer and you will easily practice all the other virtues."

Having reached the monastery, the elder offers the pilgrim instruction in prayer—guidance in using the Jesus Prayer:

> *Lord Jesus Christ, Son of God, have mercy on me,*
> *a sinner.*

This is the most familiar form of the Jesus Prayer, but it takes various forms. It can be as simple as "Lord Jesus, have mercy." It can also be adapted as a prayer for another person: "Lord Jesus, have mercy on your servant [*insert name*]." When used for others, the words "a sinner" are normally dropped. The one essential word in the prayer is "Jesus."

The roots of the prayer are in the story Jesus tells of a tax collector standing in the back of the synagogue, so ashamed of what he has done and what he has failed to do that he could hardly lift his head. All he could say was, "God, be merciful to me, a sinner!" (Luke 18:13).

In *The Way of the Pilgrim* the elder gives some basic advice about repetitive use of the Jesus Prayer:

> The continuous interior Prayer of Jesus is a constant
> uninterrupted calling upon the Divine Name of Jesus
> with the lips, in the spirit, in the heart, while forming a
> mental picture of his constant presence, and imploring

19

his grace, during every occupation, at all times, in all places, even during sleep. ... I give you my permission to say your prayer as often as you wish and as often as you can. Try to devote every moment you are awake to the prayer. Call on the Name of Jesus without counting the number of times, and submit yourself humbly to the will of God, looking to him for help.

The elder gives the pilgrim a copy of *The Philokalia,* a collection of texts written in earlier centuries by saints who were teachers of prayer. Picking a passage from the writings of Saint Simeon the New Theologian, the elder reads aloud:

Sit down alone and in silence, lower your head, shut your eyes, breathe out gently, and imagine yourself looking into your own heart. ... Let your thoughts descend from your head to your heart. As you breathe out, say, "Lord Jesus Christ, have mercy on me."

An important aspect of the Jesus Prayer is the emphasis its teachers place on the heart, which is understood not only as a muscle that pumps blood but also as the warm center of each person in which the integration of body, mind, and soul occurs.

Christ said, "Blessed are the pure of heart." In our brain-obsessed society it ought to disturb us that Christ didn't say, "Blessed are the brilliant in mind." These days most of us tend to regard the brain as the core of the self. The brain has come up in the world while the heart has been demoted. Yet even in our time, at least in metaphor, the heart is still linked with our capacity to love. We still speak of "getting to the heart of things." According to the Russian author Boris Vysheslavtsev, "The heart is the center not only of consciousness but of the unconscious, not only of the soul but of the spirit, not only of the spirit but of the body, not only of the comprehensible but of the incomprehensible; in one word, it is the absolute center."[12]

The pilgrim's providential meeting with the elder occurs early in *The Way of the Pilgrim.* Most of the book is an account of the pilgrim's experience in learning the use of the Jesus Prayer, which in time becomes an inner dimension of his walking from place to place; it gradually takes root not only in his mind but also in his heart, until it becomes as normal and primary an activity as breathing. At night the pilgrim finds himself dreaming the Jesus Prayer.

Every now and then I have the blessing of meeting someone who gives me a glimpse of a life in which prayer has become integral with the person's heartbeat. I think, for example, of a man I met at a church shop that was built into the wall of the Danilovsky Monastery in Moscow. Now that I think about it, he looked like the person I envision as author of *The Way of the Pilgrim*—a lean, grizzled man, something of a human cactus, wearing old clothing that seemed to be a record in fabric of many years of hard Russian weather.

As he gave me change for a twenty-ruble note, he was quietly whispering not numbers, it dawned on me, but a short form of the Jesus Prayer: "Jesus, have mercy." After putting the change in my pocket, I lingered a short time, pretending to look at items for sale, but really only to see if his whispered prayer ever stopped. If it did, it was not while I was there.

I doubt many people achieve the state of ceaseless prayer the Russian pilgrim sought so avidly. My own prayer is far from constant. But I also know that at any moment of the day or night the Jesus Prayer is waiting within me to be used. If sleep evades me, I can use this prayer instead of being irritated at the problem of being awake. If I am walking into town to shop, I find I am better off, and less likely to buy things, when I use the Jesus Prayer. If I am standing in line at the supermarket, instead of being annoyed that I have to wait, I can shelter myself in the Jesus Prayer. All "in-between" times have the potential of being times for the Jesus Prayer.

My wife and I know a nun living in Chicago who is devoted to the Jesus Prayer. From her we learned more about praying in crowded places. As she never got a driver's license, she travels on public buses back and forth from her convent to the university where she teaches. City buses have become for her both a means of pilgrimage and a school of prayer. She glances at faces, trying to be sensitive to whatever the face reveals—boredom, anxiety, fear, anger, love, irritation, impatience, confusion, depression, despair—all the while praying for that person. She often uses a simple variation of the Jesus prayer: "Lord Jesus Christ, have mercy [*on him, on her, on the woman in the blue blouse, on the man who is so upset, etc.*]."

"It's amazing how much faces on buses reveal," she says. Her approach is discreet—staring is out of the question. She respects the privacy of the people for whom she is praying. She calls her way of looking at others "benevolent glancing," a phrase she first encountered in a press account of Pope John Paul meeting with the Buddhist patriarch in Thailand. The first part of their encounter, it was reported, was an extended period of silence during which they exchanged "benevolent glances."

One of our modern teachers of prayer was the Dutch priest Henri Nouwen, who sometimes spoke with friends about practicing the Jesus Prayer. It was an important element of his spiritual life, but not the only one. In a book written during a five-month stay in Rome, he offered an insight about ceaseless prayer. Here his stress was not on a particular method, such as the use of a repetitive prayer, but on an ever-deepening consciousness of knowing that every action and every thought occurs in the presence of God, an awareness that makes life an act of continuous dialogue:

To pray . . . does not mean to think about God in contrast to thinking about other things, or to spend time with God instead of spending time with other people. Rather, it means to think and live in the presence of God. As soon as we begin to divide our thoughts about God and thoughts about people and events, we remove God from our daily life and put him into a pious little niche where we can think pious thoughts and experience pious feelings. Although it is important and even indispensable for the spiritual life to set apart time for God and God alone, prayer can only become unceasing prayer when all our thoughts—beautiful or ugly, high or low, proud or shameful, sorrowful or joyful—can be thought in the presence of God. . . . Thus, converting our unceasing thinking into unceasing prayer moves us from a self-centered monologue to a God-centered dialogue.[13]

Particular methods of prayer can be helpful, but no method is essential. After all, prayer is something we all were born to do—and indeed are likely to do in times of stress or crisis without instruction or prodding. Making prayer a normal part of daily life, an activity as ordinary as walking or breathing, takes discipline. Yet what a different life one discovers when prayer becomes part of the basic structure of daily life, with time given to prayer at the beginning and end of each day, with islands of prayer, however brief, in between. Daily life becomes an event of pilgrimage.

The Other Side of Silence

If we had a keen vision and feeling of all ordinary human life, it would be like hearing the grass grow and the squirrel's heartbeat, and we should die of that roar which lies on the other side of silence. As it is, the quickest of us walk about well wadded with stupidity.

—GEORGE ELIOT, *MIDDLEMARCH*

There are times when good words are to be left unsaid out of esteem for silence.

—SAINT BENEDICT, THE HOLY RULE

We cannot find God in noise or agitation. Nature: trees, flowers, and grass grow in silence. The stars, the moon, and the sun move in silence.

—MOTHER TERESA OF CALCUTTA

*Voices. Voices. Listen, my heart, as only
saints have listened: until the gigantic call lifted them
off the ground; yet they kept on, impossibly,
kneeling and didn't notice at all:
so complete was their listening. Not that you could
    endure
God's voice—far from it. But listen to the voice of the
    wind
and the ceaseless message that forms itself out of silence.*

—RAINER MARIA RILKE, "DUINO ELEGIES"

*O*ne of the hallmarks of pilgrimage is an attitude of silence and attentive listening, a state of being for which few of us are well equipped. We have been shaped by a society in which noise is normal and its absence disorienting.

If our medieval ancestors were to visit us, perhaps the biggest shock that the world of the third millennium would pose for them would be the unrelenting noise that most of us endure. The noise of traffic. The noise of sirens. The noise of jet planes overhead. The noise of television and radio. The noise of machinery. The noise of overly loud conversation. The canned music pumped out of loudspeakers in so many stores. The thin, ghostly sounds emitted by earphones. The noises made by mobile phones as they announce incoming calls, followed by the noise of one-way conversations.

We live in a world in which millions of people have not only acclimated themselves to noise but become sound addicts. Many of us depend on continuous noise. For almost any urban person, silence is a stunning experience. For many, it is frightening. We all know people who keep a radio, television, or music player on continually. I recall a friend in New York who lost his job as a radio announcer on a popular station for broadcasting ten seconds of silence. His station manager said that, more than anything else, the audience depended on the station to provide constant sound. Even one second of silence meant listener distress and an urgent search for sound on another station.

Part of the asceticism of being a pilgrim is to search out places that encourage inner quietness and contemplative listening: churches, concerts, plays, museums, woods and parks, remote places, wilderness areas, monasteries, beaches, and deserts.

Silence is not silent. It is more than the absence of noise. If you manage to escape the cacophony of urban life, you quickly discover that nature isn't tongue-tied. There is a torrent of sound even at midnight on the driest, most remote desert: breezes scraping the sand, the tireless conversation of insects, the tidal sound of one's own breathing, the drumming of one's heart, the roar of being. What a pilgrim's walk can provide is the silence that comes from doing without sound-generating devices, being attentive rather than speaking, praying rather than engaging in chatter. So long as our heart keeps beating, we will never experience absolute silence, but by avoiding distractions and listening to what remains, we discover that the door to silence is everywhere, even in Times Square and Piccadilly Circus. To listen is always an act of being silent.

Finding places of relative silence can help a pilgrim discover inner silence. As the poet Bob Lax, who in his later years made his home on the quiet Greek island of Patmos, once put it in a letter to a friend:

> The thing to do with nature . . . is to listen to it, and watch it, and look deep into its eyes in a sense, as though you were listening to and watching a friend, not just hearing the words or even just watching the gestures but trying to guess, or get a sense, or share the spirit underneath it, trying to listen (if this isn't too fancy) to the silence under the sound and trying to get an idea (not starting with any preconceived formulation) of what kind of silence it is.[14]

There are as many kinds of silence as there are varieties of snow. Some forms of silence are of God's own making. Others are hostile to the spiritual life. Starting at the icy end of the spectrum, here is my list:

Deadly silence: This is the almost murderous silence of people who refuse to speak to a spouse, a parent, a child, or a neighbor; it is silence used as a weapon, silence meant to annihilate. One often witnesses it in teenagers in that period when nearly everything a parent says or does inspires homicidal glares. Not everyone outgrows it. Many a marriage has died of deadly silences.

Guilty silence: These are times when our failure to speak makes us silent collaborators in injustice or cruelty.

Ominous silence: This is the intimidating, belittling silence of a teacher or boss waiting for you to respond to a question he or she knows you cannot—or dare not—answer.

Proud silence: This is the malignant silence of the person who regards himself or herself as too important to speak to lesser mortals, at the same time communicating the message that the other, being so insignificant, had best shut up.

Anxious silence: This is the silence of fear, the silence of the paralyzed tongue. You are in the presence of someone with power over you, and you find yourself dumb. Or you are face to face with someone famous and find your tongue has turned to wood.

Awkward silence: This is the strained, embarrassed silence of being with strangers and not having a clue what to say.

Graveyard silence: A silence in which nothing makes as much noise as your own heartbeat. There is also the silence of the tomb, where every conversation has been interrupted by terror, calamity, or death.

Meek silence: This is the silence of respect, modesty, and humility. It is not bad advice to keep silent unless what you have to say is more interesting than silence.

Dumbfounded silence: This is the silence of awe—an awareness of the presence of God, of fathomless mystery, of the unspeakably beautiful.

Consoling silence: Faced with suffering or bereavement, words seem both inadequate and profane. What one has to say is best said with the eyes, tears, and mute gestures.

Enamored silence: The silence of love. No words seem equal to what you want to say. Each word or phrase you think of saying sounds like the dull noise of counterfeit coins.

Prayerful silence: This is a silence attentive to God's presence, a human silence that participates in the divine silence. It is a silence that marks many experienced pilgrims.

Last but not least, *evangelical silence*: The Greek word for the gospel is *evangelion*–good news. There are times when silence is better than words in communicating the truths that are ultimately beyond the reach of words. In a world of constant noise and endless verbal disputes, silence can sometimes communicate truths that are beyond assertion and argument.

A story of evangelical silence: Archbishop Theophilus of Alexandria, one of the principal cities of the ancient world, once traveled to the monastic colony at Skete in the Egyptian desert. The younger monks were distressed that their elder, Abbot Pambo, had nothing to say to their august and powerful visitor. "Say a word or two to the bishop," they urged him, "that his soul may be edified in this place." Abbot Pambo replied: "If he is not edified by my silence, there is no hope that he will be edified by my words."[15]

One can imagine that Archbishop Theophilus, a man who had heard endless words from the many people courting his attention, returned to Alexandria shaken by his encounter with a community of men who had completely resigned from chatter. The monks made no effort to convince him of anything or win any favors. For the length of his stay, their exalted guest was simply a fellow Christian who, in a climate of silence, found himself freed from the heavy burden of being an "important person" with all the words and gestures that importance involves. He was a visitor in a household of tranquil prayer. The monks bathed him in their own quietness.

One of the early saints who emphasized the place of silence in spiritual life was Saint Ignatius, bishop of Antioch, who died a martyr late in the first century. In a letter written shortly before his death, he wrote, "He who possesses in truth the word of Jesus can hear even its silence."[16]

Far from being a God who insists on being heard, overpowering the noise of the world with a heavenly roar, our Creator seems chiefly to speak to us so quietly that the normal environment for hearing is inner silence. The prophet Elijah experienced God's voice as a whisper. Elijah was hiding in a cave near what later became the city of Haifa. God made himself known to Elijah not in a rock-shattering wind, or in an earthquake, or in fire and lightning, but in "a still small voice" (1 Kgs 19:12).

The benefits of silence were stressed by Saint Anthony the Great, the founder of desert monasticism:

> When you lie down on your bed, remember with thanksgiving the blessings and providence of God. Thereupon, filled with good thoughts, you will rejoice in spirit and the sleep of your body will mean sobriety of the soul; the closing of your eyes a true acknowledging of God, and your silence, brimming with awareness of all that is good, will wholeheartedly and with all its strength glorify almighty God, so that praise will rise to the heavens from your heart.

Another desert saint, John Climacus, a sixth-century abbot of St. Catherine's Monastery in the barren wilderness of Sinai, stressed the role of silence in prayer in his guidebook to the spiritual life, *The Ladder of Divine Ascent:*

> Intelligent silence is the mother of prayer, freedom from bondage, custodian of zeal, a guard on our thoughts, a

watch on our enemies, a prison of mourning, a friend of tears, a sure recollection of death, a painter of punishment, a concern with judgment, servant of anguish, foe of license, a companion of stillness, the opponent of dogmatism, a growth of knowledge, a hand to shape contemplation, hidden progress, the secret journey upward.[17]

Silence is not something that can be measured with scientific instruments; nor does it exclude all conversation. Spoken words can communicate divine silence just as silence can be a voice of enmity. As another of the great desert saints, Abba Poemen the Shepherd, said:

One man seems silent of speech, but is condemning other people within his heart—he is really talking incessantly. Another man seems to talk all day, yet keeps his silence, for he always speaks in a way that is useful to his hearers.

No community of people is more aware than poets of the limitations of words. In a letter to a younger poet, Rainer Maria Rilke wrote:

Things aren't all so tangible and sayable as people would usually have us believe. Most experiences are unsayable. They happen in a space that no word has ever entered.[18]

Silence is an essential dimension of icons, which serve as wordless translations of the gospel. It is part of what distinguishes iconography from ordinary painting. Just as many paintings create an illusion of three dimensions, so can an artist suggest sound, even an eruption of noise. Stand attentively before a painting of a great battle done by a skilled

Icon given to Thomas Merton by Marco Pallis

artist and you can hear the explosions, the clash of weapons, the cries of wounded soldiers. Stand before an icon, and you find yourself enveloped in deep silence, a silence that seems to contain the breath of the Holy Spirit. Take enough time and a good icon will help quiet your mind. As you move beyond intellectual exploration of an icon's content, it may awaken a longing to pray. It may even assist you in resolving a problem you have been struggling with.

As Thomas Merton wrote to his Greek friend Marco Pallis, thanking him for the gift of a hand-painted icon:

> How shall I begin? I have never received such a precious and magnificent gift from anyone in my life. I have no words to express how deeply moved I was to come face to face with this sacred and beautiful presence granted to me. . . . At first I could hardly believe it. . . . It is a perfect act of timeless worship. I never tire of gazing at it. There is a spiritual presence and reality

about it, a true spiritual "Taboric" light, which seems unaccountably to proceed from the Heart of the Virgin and Child as if they had One heart, and which goes out to the whole universe. It is unutterably splendid. And silent. It imposes a silence on the whole hermitage. . . . [This] icon of the Holy Mother came as a messenger at a precise moment when a message was needed, and her presence before me has been an incalculable aid in resolving a difficult problem.[19]

Merton brought an icon with him on what proved to be his final journey, his pilgrimage to Asia in 1968. Though traveling light, like so many pilgrims before him, he regarded an icon as essential baggage. He knew from repeated experience that icons radiate a "Taboric" light—an intimation of the uncreated light the three apostles experienced on Galilee's Mount Tabor when the transfigured Christ silently revealed to them his divinity.

Merton's journey in the final weeks of his life was a time of silence and prayer, except in those brief periods when he was in conversation, and even then, prayer shaped the conversations. How appropriate that the few material possessions shipped back with his body included his beloved icon of Christ and his mother. "Traveling" icons—small icons mounted on cardboard or a thin piece of wood, or relief icons cast from bronze or some other metal—are part of the pilgrim tradition.

A pilgrimage without prayer is no pilgrimage at all. There is no prayer without silent, attentive listening. The invitational silence of an icon helps the pilgrim to keep praying. Place an icon next to your bed at night. In the daytime be aware of it in your pocket or backpack. It provides a quiet but insistent reminder of what the journey is all about.

Pilgrimage is an hour-by-hour school of inner listening that combines movement with seeing, attentiveness, and prayer. Whether on the way to the market or on the way to Jerusalem, you see whatever there is to see: other people, traffic, garbage, flowers, weeds, wildlife, the natural world. You hear all the sounds the world around you is pronouncing: bird songs, the wind, cars, buses, trucks, planes overhead, the conversation of people along the way, the sound of your feet on various surfaces. Little that you see will imprint itself as a long-term memory. Most that you hear will come in one ear and go out the other. Mainly what we see and hear as pilgrims passes through us like light passing through glass, yet to pay attention is to be in a moment-to-moment state of communion.

Prayer, too, is rarely remembered. It is the unusual event, not the routine, that carves a place in memory. Prayer, to the extent that it becomes ordinary, is no more memorable than breathing.

I recall a conversation about silence with our daughter Wendy when she was four or five years old. She said, "You know what those little sounds are that you hear when you're all alone?"

"What sounds?" I asked.

"You know, those sounds you hear when you're alone."

"What's that, Wendy?" I replied.

"That's God," she said.

Psalter Mappa Mundi

Maps

If you see a whole thing—it seems that it's always beautiful. Planets, lives . . . But up close a world's all dirt and rocks. And day to day, life's a hard job, you get tired, you lose the pattern.

—Ursula K. Le Guin

Journey all over the universe in a map, without the expense and fatigue of traveling, without suffering the inconveniences of heat, cold, hunger, and thirst.

—Miguel de Cervantes, *Don Quixote*

We're all pilgrims on the same journey, but some pilgrims have better road maps.

—Nelson DeMille

If geography is prose, maps are iconography.

—Lennart Meri

As with roads, so with maps, we tend to take them for granted, as ordinary as wallpaper, though we find it annoying if the map maker doesn't orient the map in the right way, with north at the top. As it happens, correctly oriented maps at one time had east at the top, but whatever way a map is turned and no matter what is included and what is left out, every map is an icon. Even with the most exact renderings, every map is a work of abstract art with a heavy reliance on color and symbol. Every map portrays what the map maker thinks matters most to the viewer.

For us, maps provide detailed, practical information about how to get from here to there. On a somewhat grander scale, they serve as political-economic statements. The classroom maps I gazed at as a child put North America on top and in the center, slicing Asia in half, one side to the left, the other to the right.

A medieval map maker had different priorities. Look, for example, at the medieval *mappa mundi* (map of the world) that now resides in the British Library in London. Called the Psalter map, it was made by an unknown hand, probably in Westminster, about the year 1250. Only fifty-two inches across, this document, made for Henry III, is thought to be a copy of a much larger world map, since lost, which once hung in the Palace of Westminster.

In today's cartography, national borders–nonexistent in medieval maps–are precisely drawn, with the northern hemisphere (economically and politically dominant) on top. In contrast, the Psalter *mappa mundi* gives position of honor to the Garden of Eden.

Such pre-Columbian maps tend to strike the modern viewer as an embarrassingly primitive starting point in the long history of seeing the world as it might be viewed from the moon–circular, yes, but containing much more than medieval map makers dared imagine or sought to portray.

What mattered most to the Europeans who drew the medieval *mappa mundi* and similar maps was not to depict the exact shape of countries, continents, and oceans, but to present the known world as a unity seen through a biblical lens. A Christian medieval map was not only a graphic presentation of what map makers knew about the world, but also an image of the world in which what mattered most was not geography but salvation. The *mappa mundi* was meant to assist those who saw in it their pilgrimage toward the heavenly Jerusalem. Thus Jerusalem was placed at the center, for it was here that history's most decisive event occurred. After all, what was more significant than Christ's victory over death? The resurrection made Jerusalem the center of all points. Just as Easter was the axis around which the church's calendar turned, so Jerusalem, the city of the empty tomb, had to be the world's hub.

The Psalter *mappa mundi* is crowned by the presence of Christ presiding over the world with angels on either side—one angel solemn, the other smiling—honoring him with incense. Christ is shown iconographically as *Kyrios Pantocrator*: the Lord of Creation.

With his right hand Christ offers a gesture of blessing, while with his left he holds a small world globe that is, itself, a yet simpler map of the world. It is a circle containing a T, a simple Greek cross with Asia at the top, Africa at the lower right, and Europe at the lower left. These segments also represented the divisions of the earth allocated to the three sons of Noah—Shem, Japhet, and Ham—who after the Flood became arch-ancestors of all the world's races. The T separating the three continents signified the known world's three main waterways. The upright stem running from west eastward to the center of the world was the Mediterranean. The left half of the crossbar represented the Tanais (today called the Don), and the right half of the crossbar represented the Nile.

In fact, the Psalter map is simply an elaborated version of the T map. Both put east where, in contemporary maps, north would be. In both maps the Mediterranean Sea serves as the T's upward stroke, fed by the Don on the left and the Nile on the right. But the Psalter map is crowded with detail. Places of biblical importance are stressed. Most prominent, directly beneath the circular face at the top of the globe, is the Garden of Eden, shown as the source of five rivers. A medallion is placed in the middle of paradise, Adam on one side, Eve on the other, with the tree of knowledge dividing them.

Other biblically significant details on the map's top half include a small banana shape (Noah's ark resting on Armenia's Mount Ararat), the Red Sea (made red indeed, and showing the briefly dry path by which the Jews crossed), and walls imprisoning Gog in the land of Magog. Above Jerusalem is the Sea of Galilee, populated by the map's one fish, with the Dead Sea off to the right.

Among the map's 145 place inscriptions, many are places closer to home for the cartographer. For example, the city of Rome stands to the left of the Mediterranean, but it appears as only a minor detail. In the *mappa mundi* all roads lead to Jerusalem.

Not the least striking detail of the map is the crowd of figures shown against panels of red and black on the far side of Africa. Fourteen imagined races include dog-like folk, people with giant heads, tribes without tongues or ears, beings with four eyes, and those who don't walk but crawl on their hands and feet. All this is an iconographer's way of suggesting the drama of human otherness. Even stranger figures were carved in stone over the entrance to the basilica at Vézeley to dramatize the implications of Christ's command to his apostles that they bring the gospel to the entire world, not only to the familiar but to the unfamiliar.

Also featured on the Psalter map are twelve faces forming a necklace around the world-containing circle. These represent the winds that blow from the twelve compass points. The four red faces mark east, south, west, and north.

There are also references to medieval contemporary life, events, and economics. The inclusion of Damietta in Egypt commemorates that city's capture for the Crusade by Louis IX of France in 1249. Cologne is included, presumably because it was a major commercial and ecclesiastical center.

What maps leave out is often more interesting than what they display. When the British economist E. F. Schumacher visited Moscow in Soviet times, he was given a tourist map of the city in which major buildings and principal monuments were displayed in small drawings. Finding himself in front of a large church and not sure where he was, he searched among the various images of churches on the map to identify the one before him and thus ascertain his location, but no church on the map seemed to resemble it. At last an English-speaking passerby, seeing his confusion, stopped to assist him. He pointed out to Schumacher that the church in question, impressive though it was, did not appear on the map. "Why not?" Schumacher asked. "It's a living church," the Muscovite explained. "It's still a place of worship. Soviet maps only show dead churches—churches that have become museums."

In an atheist state, living churches are regarded as non-buildings and their occupants as non-persons. The map in Schumacher's hands reflected, as all maps do, the priorities, the world view, and even the ideology of its makers.

The maze-like *mappa mundi* is not the world globe as any school child today knows it, yet it reveals basic truths ignored by modern maps. For all that is missing or distorted in squeezing the known world into so compressed a circle, the map displays a world whose history was set in motion by choices made by one man and one woman living in a lost garden somewhere in the East. Most important, the map makes plain a world whose center point is the death and resurrection of Jesus Christ.

For a Christian pilgrim, the *mappa mundi*, for all its geographical naivete, still reveals more about what life's journey is all about than a map on a schoolroom wall.

Chartres Cathedral

Mazes

Life is a maze in which we take the wrong turn before we have learnt to walk.

—CYRIL CONNOLLY

What could be more delightful than to have in the same few minutes all the fascinating terrors of going abroad combined with all the humane security of coming home again?

—G. K. CHESTERTON, *ORTHODOXY*

What we call the beginning is often the end, and to make an end is to make a beginning. The end is where we start from.

—T. S. ELIOT

The Archangel Michael, as Henry Adams observed in *Mont Saint Michel and Chartres,* loves heights. Towering, fortress-like churches dedicated to the heavenly warrior have often been built on forbidding pinnacles of rock. The most famous, Mont Saint Michel, is poised atop a dagger of stone on the tidal flatland just off the southwest coast of Normandy near the border with Brittany. When the tide is up, the abbey is like a magnificent ship anchored offshore. Both location and architecture suggest a readiness to withstand the sieges of armies and the elements. The fortifications may have helped ward off Vikings but have also made Mont Saint Michel a major attraction for tourists and pilgrims.

The Virgin Mary seems to prefer more accessible locations. Rarely do any remarkable obstacles impede the pilgrim's way. Take the example of the Cathedral of Our Lady at Chartres, one of the most important centers of pilgrimage in Europe, whose town is set amid a vast moat of wheat fields.

There has been a church in Chartres dedicated to Christ's mother since at least the fourth century, when Saint Adventinus was the local bishop. Stone masons have labored on the site again and again. Work on the main part of the present church began in 1194 after a fire destroyed a smaller cathedral. Thanks in large measure to the many thousands of pilgrims who came annually to make a gift of their labor, most of the construction was finished by 1230. The cathedral at Chartres is not only a goal of pilgrimage but a work of pilgrimage.

These days most pilgrims arrive in Chartres by train, car, or bicycle, but even in secular, postmodern Europe there are those who still make the journey on foot. No matter what their mode of travel, pilgrims look eagerly toward the horizon waiting for the gray profile of the cathedral to rise above the grain. For those traveling in groups, there is often a spire-spotting contest. When we were traveling by rented car on our last visit to Chartres, our daughter Anne won a coin for being first to spot those two arrow-sharp towers.

Approaching Chartres through the wide plain of surrounding fields, the hill on which the town and cathedral are built gradually reveals itself. From every vantage point the cathedral dominates the view, its two great towers rising heavenward from the heart of the town. The cathedral's spires have a magnetic strength, compelling the pilgrim to make no other stop before reaching the church and entering the western doors—the Royal Portal—that stand between the towers.

Stepping inside the church, the pilgrim stands within a vast enclosure that seems to be an entrance point to the kingdom of God. The immense, softly lit, column-lined space is a domain in which ordinary time hardly exists and doesn't matter. One's first impression is of a tremendous silence, even among whispered conversations or a softly chanted Mass. The 176 windows–among the best preserved medieval glass the world possesses–are a Bible written in fragments of colored glass. Reds and blues are the most dominant, the colors of ice and fire. Others play supporting roles: deep forest green, pale lilac, lemon yellow, all enhanced by ebony lines glazed onto the glass to provide image details and the black tracery of lead connecting the pieces.

Those who are drawn to Chartres, whether they see themselves as pilgrims or simply as tourists, often spend many hours "reading" the windows panel by panel and derive the satisfaction of breaking a code as they work out the meaning of each. Camping on the edge of town, as our family did during our last visit to Chartres, we stopped one morning at a local camera shop to buy a pair of binoculars, eager to get closer to the glass. We wondered if our ancestors, who read less or not at all, might not have had better eyes for distance vision and thus found it easier to decipher the glasswork.

The windows are a kind of giant puzzle for the eyes and mind. Little by little one sees how all the panels connect–how the story in one panel is threaded to the next, each window in dialogue with its neighbors.

"It's a giant comic book," our daughter Anne commented. She was right, so long as one understands "comic" not as a synonym for "funny," but in the sense of Dante's divine comedy.

At the heart of the cathedral, as in every church with a eucharistic tradition, is its main altar. Each altar is a center of the universe. Each altar is a table of divine hospitality. The altar is a place where a frequent miracle occurs–bread and wine become the body and blood of Christ. Christ is both hidden and revealed in the most basic of foods.

At the foot of the central aisle that leads toward the main altar is a treasure that visitors often walk over without noticing: a circular maze. It is the cathedral's most abstract work of art and the only one designed as much for the feet as for the eye. The mosaic maze is more than thirteen yards from edge to edge, the width of the pillar-bordered avenue that leads to the altar.

Unlike the labyrinth in ancient Crete, where the hero Theseus conquered the Minotaur and cleverly found his way out by following the thread given him by Ariadne, the maze at Chartres is not life-threatening. Its "walls," traced in black stone, rise only in the imagination. The unicursal path of white stone has no blind alleys, traps, pits, dead ends, or secret chambers. If you wish, there is nothing to stop you from walking straight to the center without bothering to follow the path, but something deeply rooted in human nature makes even the casual visitor carefully follow the white track, treating the black lines as impassable barriers. An occasional pilgrim makes the journey on penitential knees, but the majority walk upright. Either way, it is a reassuring experience. While there are many twists and turns, with the pilgrim often being led away from the goal, whoever stays on the path ultimately reaches the center.

The unicursal journey, with all its detours, condenses the lifelong quest to achieve union with God. It is a simple model of each person's journey of faith. The center represents the most holy of pilgrimage goals: Jerusalem.

Even if pilgrims cannot lose their way in the Chartres maze, what appears at first glance to be a simple walk within a circle shows itself to be the way of the cross. The path's many turnings occur around a cruciform pattern. The maze entrance—symbolic of baptism—seems to lead directly to the center but then abruptly branches off to the left. Then, where the left arm of the cross would be, the path doubles back, soon returning the walker to the path heading toward the center, but instead only grazes the innermost circle before going outward again. One reaches the maze's center point—Jerusalem with its empty tomb—only after making a grand tour of the entire circle, with all its sudden turns, a process achieved simply by carefully placing one foot in front of the other, staying on the path, making turns that form the pattern of the life-giving cross.

The maze at Chartres is circular. The circle—a line without beginning or end—is a symbol of eternity. The same symbol is used in Christian iconography to form the halo, the sign that someone has become whole: a new person transformed in Christ-revealing, self-giving love and, united with Christ, now experiencing eternal life.

The circular, cross-containing maze is a simple map of the path to sanctity, a wordless image of the New Testament. Its message: Follow the path of the gospel, and the mercy of God will finally bring you to the heavenly Jerusalem, the kingdom of God, no matter how many turns you make along the way or how many times your goal may seem to recede. Along the way you will discover, and even carry, the cross, but the cross contains the resurrection—life with Christ and all the saints in the new Jerusalem.

Relics

We do not worship relics any more than we do the sun or moon, the angels, archangels, or seraphim. We honor them in honor of Him whose faith the saints gave witness. We honor the Master by means of his servants.

—Saint Jerome

Like Roman Catholics, Orthodox Christians believe that the grace of God present in the saints' bodies during life remains active in their relics when they have died, and that God uses these relics as a channel of divine power, as an instrument of healing.

—Bishop Kallistos Ware, *The Orthodox Church*

The cult of relics was at the heart of pilgrimage, so, walking as I was in medieval footsteps, I was curious to understand something of their power, to know how they would have been a source of forgiveness, guidance and healing. But to do so I would have to bury my prejudices.

—Shirley du Boulay, *The Road to Canterbury*

*W*herever relics are kept, you find people praying, and not just in their minds but with their bodies, kneeling or prostrate. There is a powerful sense of heaven and earth rubbing against each other.

It wasn't the magnificent church building or the wonderful stained glass that brought so many thousands of pilgrims

46

to Chartres in earlier ages. It was the cathedral's most famous relic, the *Sancta Camisia*. According to tradition, this was a garment Mary was wearing when she gave birth to Jesus and may have been wearing at the time of the annunciation. This ancient rectangle of translucent, ivory-colored fabric has been a powerful magnet throughout the cathedral's life.

Medieval church documents record that the relic was given in the year 876 to Charlemagne's grandson, Charles the Bald, by Byzantine Empress Irene. Charles, in turn, entrusted it to the monks at Chartres.

Just thirty-five years later, in 911, Chartres was besieged by the Viking chieftain Rollon. The town's bishop in those days, Gantelmne, responded by displaying the *Sancta Camisia*

Sancta Camisia from Chartres

on the city wall. Apparently the sight of so famous and powerful a relic was enough to give even a Viking second thoughts. Not only was the siege lifted, but Rollon was baptized the following year. Later he was made Duke of Normandy by King Charles III of France. William the Conqueror, an ancestor of the present British royal family, was among Rollon's descendants.

The *Sancta Camisia* has survived long journeys, the rise and fall of empires, Viking attacks, fires, and wars down to the present day, but the French Revolution might well have been the end of both the relic and its cathedral. During the last decade of the eighteenth century, revolutionaries in Chartres sought to use the great church as a stone quarry. While the guillotine was hard at work removing heads in Paris, the cathedral in Chartres awaited its own execution. Pilgrims today owe a great debt to all those local citizens who, risking their lives, managed to save the church and its most prized relic from the ideological hurricanes of those years.

The *Sancta Camisia* is kept in the oldest part of the cathedral, the crypt, directly beneath the upper church's high altar.

Relics are important in both the Orthodox and Catholic churches. In both traditions no altar is regarded as complete without them.

Pilgrims tend to be people who value relics and seek them out with reverence, but these days many visitors to churches that exhibit relics regard such items with raised eyebrows and condescending smiles. Such skepticism is widespread in our culture.

Standing in the crypt at Chartres, I overheard a man saying to his wife: "How do they know this is the real thing? How do they know this isn't just some fragment of old cloth that was passed off as a relic centuries ago by a con man whose only interest was moving money from other pockets into his own?"

"Yes, I suppose," his wife replied, adding, "You know, if all the bits of cloth that were supposedly worn by Mary were gathered together, you would have enough fabric to make a circus tent."

Her husband then switched to the dismissive approach: "And anyway, even if it is authentic, a relic is, after all, just what it is, nothing more. So what if it was something Mary wore? Big deal. You might as well pray before one of my old tee-shirts."

Yet for all the hesitations and outright scoffing when it comes to saints' relics, even the most secularized skeptics turn out to have an interest in relics, so long as they connect with a person or event that excites their interest.

Tell your friend that a certain film star sat in a certain chair in your living room, and your friend will forever after regard that chair in a slightly different light and may even prefer sitting there.

Put a pair of sparkly red shoes on sale with a tag identifying them as having been worn by Judy Garland when she was playing Dorothy in "The Wizard of Oz" and eyes widen. Should you have a certificate of authenticity from the film studio, you'll find those old battered shoes have suddenly become more valuable than your house.

You might have a dull gray chunk of concrete on your fireplace mantle, but mention it was once part of the Berlin Wall and an otherwise prosaic item suddenly is part of a story that makes it shine in the dark.

Even signatures can become treasures to us—a painting signed by Picasso will fetch a higher price than a painting Picasso neglected to sign. Experts command hefty fees just for verifying that the artist's signature is real.

Elvis Presley is long dead, but his home in Memphis, Tennessee, is the goal of a daily river of devoted fans. When the Japanese prime minister, Junichiro Koizumi, visited Graceland in 2006, he was deeply moved to be given a transparent plastic envelope with a cutting of Presley's hair.

Every day long lines of pilgrims wind their way through rooms that Elvis lived in. Not long ago my friend Paul Chandler, a Carmelite priest, was among them. He writes:

> I made it to Memphis and to the Presley mansion and did the Graceland tour (Platinum Package, $24). I stood in the garden at Elvis' grave, slightly bemused by the large number of people sobbing. A big, dignified man with his arm around his weeping wife gave me a nod. I nodded gravely back, not entirely sure of what was passing between us, but knowing that something was. . . .
>
> There are interesting things to see in Graceland, which is pretty much as the King left it. You can see the Jungle Room (Elvis had no taste in furniture), the kitchen where they cooked up his favorite deep-fried peanut butter sandwiches, his two private jets, a collection of satin and rhinestone jumpsuits, and the TV set he shot a bullet into one night when he was tired and emotional and they were a bit slow getting the gun away from him.
>
> I thought it was well worth the platinum ticket. For some odd reason I best remember incidental things from my big trip to Graceland: a kindness here, a nod there, a fear disarmed, a prejudice undone.
>
> People have been going to visit St. James in Compostela since the ninth century . . . and they have been going to Graceland to visit Elvis since 1977. . . . Why does the dead Elvis still call travelers to Memphis, and St. James to Compostela? What kind of journey makes you a pilgrim and not just a traveler?
>
> You can be a traveler on your own, but not, I think, a pilgrim. Pilgrimage connects you to something bigger

than yourself. Pilgrimage connects you to longings that come from deep places and that cannot be easily explained. Even the solitary pilgrim is on a shared quest, overhearing some whisper of a conversation that has been going on for years. Pilgrims don't always have a clear idea of what they're doing or why they're doing it, but they keep going, exchanging nods on the way. Their touch can wear away stone.

Grace is subtle and elusive. You're not a pilgrim if you stay where you are.

If the homes of dead rock stars touch the hearts of many people, how much more significant are those things—whether a fragment of Mary's clothing or a splinter of the true cross or a paper signed by a saint or a fragment of a martyr's body—that connect us to people whose love of God and neighbor changed the world?

In the early church the remains of people who were martyred were buried with care and immediately became gathering places of prayer. Human beings haven't changed. Relics help make real what before may have seemed merely mythological. They deepen relationships between us and those who have gone before us. They provide threads that help us find our way through life's maze. Surprisingly often, saints' relics are linked to events of miraculous healing for pilgrims.

My first encounter with the relics of a saint's body occurred in Novgorod, Russia, in the winter of 1987. *Novgorod* means "new town," which was true about eleven hundred years ago. It's a city dense with ancient churches, seventy-seven of them in all, wonderful to look at, though in Soviet days only a few remained active places of worship. In earlier times, when it was one of the principal cities of Russia, the city was known as Lord Novgorod the Great. Its circular kremlin, called the *Detinets*, stands on an embankment above the Volkhov River, with the Market Town on the facing bank. The present fortress wall of red brick was put up in the 1480s. In the center is the Cathedral of St. Sophia–Holy Wisdom. Its six towers are topped with green helmet-shaped cupolas. My host in Novgorod was Fr. Michael. I doubt I have ever seen a more Russian face: pale skin, high forehead, hair combed straight back, the bone behind his eyebrows very pronounced, slate-blue eyes, huge hands. He was mightily built, with a body worthy of a bear. He had been born in 1924. In 1944 he was seriously wounded while fighting on the White Russian Front. After the war he studied at the Leningrad Theological Seminary. When I met him, he had been a priest for nearly forty years, most of them in Novgorod, "a city," he said, "of churches, legends and saints."

Fr. Michael was a man with a passionate spirit. "People listen with their ears," he told me, "but they feel with their hearts. They know if Christ is in you or not."

We visited his parish, the Church of Saints Nicholas and Philip, founded in the twelfth century. Originally these were two adjacent churches facing different streets, but somehow they became one, growing into a single structure like an old married couple. They were shining white, with shingled onion domes, wide log porches with rough wood stairs leading up to them, and two icons set into the outer walls of the church. Trudging through deep snow, the candle-lit icons were fireplaces of warmth and invitation.

Sometimes the inside of an old church isn't as beautiful as the outside, but here the two are well matched, in part thanks to a new iconostasis made in the sixteenth-century style, the work of contemporary artists from Palekh. The dominating colors are mustard yellow, a thick creamy white, dark red, and dark green. There is no gold or silver overlay. In the twentieth century, artists in the village of Palekh, northeast of Moscow, became renowned for painting scenes from Russian legends and fairy tales on little boxes and brooches, many of which are now in museums. Before the revolution, Palekh was a famous center for painting icons. In the 1980s, the final decade of the Soviet Union, some of the village artisans were at last able to revive Palekh's earlier tradition.

The main treasure of the church, Fr. Michael pointed out, is not its icons, but a relic, the body of Saint Nikita, at one time the bishop of Novgorod, who died early in the twelfth century. It has long been a place of prayer and veneration for pilgrims.

"Would you like to venerate Saint Nikita?" Fr. Michael asked me.

I must have said yes, or at least nodded my head, because Fr. Michael lifted the coffin's glass lid so that I could kiss the thin silk veil that covers the saint's face.

This was a startling experience for me. Kissing a dead body was not something I had ever done before. More from courtesy than courage I managed to overcome my resistance only to discover that, far from inhaling the smell of death, a sweet fragrance was arising from this ancient corpse. Somehow both familiar and unnameable, the experience gave new meaning to the phrase "the odor of sanctity."[20]

Pilgrims tend to be people who have overcome the temptation to regard relics with suspicion. They reckon that, in most cases, those who found and preserved relics were people who were careful about the truth and were well aware that committing fraud is a grave sin. Lying has never been a plus for anyone hoping to get into heaven. And if mistakes were sometimes made, or deceptions arranged by people driven by greed, no matter. God will regard the pilgrim's reverence for a relic as veneration for what it represents rather than what it is.

Saints of Pilgrimage

We are all called to be saints.

—SAINT PAUL

There is but one sadness . . . and that is for us not to be saints.

—LEON BLOY, *THE WOMAN WHO WAS POOR*

Saints are not canonized for the excellence of their intellects but for the excellence of their lives.

—KENNETH WOODWARD, *MAKING SAINTS*

We are formed by what we admire. But it is possible to cultivate one's taste in this regard as in any other pursuit. It is important to learn how to recognize what is good, to train our ears to discern the truth, to pay honor to what is truly honorable, to choose a moral standard that lies beyond our easy grasp. It is especially important to convey such lessons to our children, who are otherwise too easily beguiled by our culture to admire what is merely glib or successful, to honor power, superficial beauty, and the illusion of celebrity.

—ROBERT ELLSBERG, *ALL SAINTS*

"The history of saints is mainly the history of insane people." So said Italian dictator Benito Mussolini. He was onto something. The priorities that give direction to a saint's life often seem to belong to a person who is not playing with a full deck of cards.

But is it such a blessing to be regarded as sane? It is striking that during Adolf Eichmann's trial for presiding over Hitler's death camps a psychiatrist reported that he had found Eichmann to be "perfectly sane." But then again, why is this surprising? It seems mass murder–such events as the fire storms created by the bombings of Dresden and Hiroshima or the administration of concentration camps–is never committed by people who might be regarded as out of touch with reality. Those who issue orders for annihilation, and those who carry out such orders, turn out to be paragons of what passes for sanity in the "real world."

By "real world" standards can saints be regarded as sane? Probably not. No one has ever been canonized for being sensible. No one has been placed on the calendar of the saints for killing people or for developing new, more powerful weapons. No saint devoted his or her life to accumulating wealth or political power. No halo has been placed over the head of those who drove the poor from their homes. Reading the lives of the saints, one finds people who lived in poverty, served the homeless, devoted their lives to prayer, withdrew from worldly society, died rather than compromise their faith, and in other ways went in what most "sensible" people would regard as the wrong direction–the direction of folly and madness. No wonder so many saints have been called crazy by their more level-headed, prudent neighbors. As Ralph Waldo Emerson wrote, "The virtues of society are the vices of the saints."

Each saint's life is a drama of pilgrimage in which being in the kingdom of God is a daily goal.

Such pilgrimage need not involve travel. Even a saint who lived the greater part of his or her life in a monastery, never going outside the gate, was on a constant journey. But there are saints whose lives involved much travel and may be seen, in a double sense, as pilgrim saints.

Christianity's most famous pilgrim saint is surely Saint Paul, who crisscrossed the Roman Empire as a tireless missionary and wrote a series of letters that became a major part of the New Testament. There is no other saint of the early church about whom we know so much.

Paul was born at Tarsus in Cilicia (southeastern Turkey in the modern world), the son of a Roman citizen, and grew up in a pious Jewish family associated with the Pharisaic tradition. At the time of his circumcision, eight days after he was born, he was given the name Saul in memory of the first king of the Jews. As a Roman citizen he was given the Latin name Paul. Growing up, he learned the trade of tent making. For his religious education he was sent to Jerusalem to study in the school of Gamaliel, one of the greatest teachers in the annals of Judaism. It was because of Gamaliel's advice to his fellow members of the Sanhedrin that Saint Peter

and the other apostles were not put to death for preaching the gospel.

In contrast to his teacher, Paul was at first a passionate opponent of the movement associated with Jesus. He was present when Stephen, the first deacon, was stoned to death in Jerusalem. Afterward, on his way to Damascus to help repress the local Christian community, he had an encounter with the risen Christ. He heard the words, "Saul,

Saul, why do you persecute me?" In his meeting with Christ, Paul was struck blind.

Arriving at last in Damascus, Paul went to a Christian home where he was welcomed, baptized, and recovered his sight. He began to preach in the local synagogues that Christ is the Son of God. No longer an enemy of Christ's disciples but rather a powerful ally, he was now among those facing persecution.

It was Paul who first saw Christians as pilgrims simply by virtue of their conversion and its implications, for all who follow Christ "desire a better country, that is, a heavenly one. Therefore God is not ashamed to be called their God; indeed, he has prepared a city for them" (Heb 11:16). Thus we are a pilgrim people, always on our way but, while we live in this damaged world, never arriving.

For the rest of his life Paul was one of the most effective advocates of Christ and the founder of many local churches, traveling great distances and suffering shipwreck, physical abuse, and imprisonment, until finally he was beheaded in Rome during the reign of Nero.

Paul's numerous pilgrimage journeys were not to places made sacred by past events in Jewish or Christian history but to places that became sacred because of what he achieved in bringing so many people to faith.

"It is no longer I who live," he wrote in one of his many letters, "but it is Christ who lives in me" (Gal 2:20).

One of the early saints of pilgrimage was Saint Helena, mother of the emperor Constantine and one of the patron saints of pilgrimage. She was born in the mid-third century. According to Saint Ambrose of Milan, her father was an innkeeper. It was only in her old age that she found her way to Christianity and was baptized. According to testimony written soon after her death, her conversion had a profound impact on her way of life. She often participated in church services, always dressed in modest and plain attire, was generous to the poor and eager to serve them, freed many slaves, and provided encouragement and financial support for the building of numerous churches.

The final great act of her life was to go on pilgrimage to the Holy Land. It was the year 326. She was about seventy-five years old. According to an account by Rufinus, while in Jerusalem she was distressed to find the place of Christ's death and resurrection buried beneath a pagan temple dedicated to Aphrodite. According to Saint Jerome, the temple had been constructed at the orders of the Emperor Hadrian precisely to obliterate the memory of Christ. With the cooperation of Saint Macarius, bishop of the city, Helena arranged the removal of the temple and the rubble beneath it so that a Christian basilica could be erected. No doubt it helped that she was the emperor's mother; no ordinary pilgrim would have been able to arrange the destruction of an existing temple.

In September 326, Christians living in Jerusalem assisted her in finding the cross on a spot adjacent to Golgotha, a former water cistern. Not one but several crosses were discovered. To which of them had Christ been nailed? According to one account, a critically ill woman was asked to lie upon each cross. On one of them she was healed. In this way the true cross was recognized.

Helena's death seems to have occurred in the year 330, for the last coins stamped with her name bear that date. Her body was brought to Constantinople and laid to rest in the Church of the Apostles. Her tomb soon became a place of pilgrimage. She is one of the saints who, in the Orthodox Church, is regarded as an equal of the apostles. It is rare to find an Orthodox church without her icon.

Perhaps the most famous saint of Spain, a land especially linked with pilgrimage, is Teresa of Jesus. She was born in 1515 in Avila, a Spanish hilltop town whose massive medieval walls survive to the present day. Her birth occurred only a generation after the army of Ferdinand and Isabella had defeated the Moors in Grenada. For the first time in eight hundred years Spain was a Catholic kingdom, but one in which the place of those descended from non-Catholic families, whether Muslim or Jewish, was far from secure. As a result, Teresa's family, though devout Catholics, carefully hid its Jewish roots.

By the time she was twenty Teresa had decided to become a nun, but her father had other plans for his vivacious daughter. Teresa, more than her father's equal in willfulness, secretly ran off to the Carmelite Convent of the Incarnation in Avila. Yet the convent she had joined was far from inspiring as a place of prayer and ascetic life. The once-demanding Carmelite rule had been relaxed in so many ways that the community had become a comfortable hotel in which the nuns from more affluent families were waited on by those of more humble origins.

At the age of thirty-nine, as she gazed at an image of the suffering Christ on the cross, Teresa experienced a profound conversion. She found herself overwhelmed by a sense of dismay for the tattered state of her prayer life and the many comforts and indulgences she had come to take for granted. Devoting herself to a life of active prayer, she began to have vivid experiences of God's love and presence.

Her mystical encounters with Christ inspired a longing to found a reformed Carmelite community in which the sisters would embrace the primitive rule of Carmel. After strenuous lobbying both with town and church authorities, she at last won permission to make a small foundation. Her new convent, dedicated to Saint Joseph, opened its doors in Avila in 1562. It was unique in many ways, but most of all for the community's poverty. As a matter of principle, Teresa had decided the convent would have no financial endowments. The sisters were to live a simple life supported not by donations but by their own labor.

In 1567 Teresa received a patent from the head of the Carmelite order to establish new houses. Thus she who did so much to encourage an enclosed and hidden life became an almost constant traveler. Between 1567 and 1571 she founded sixteen reformed convents. Truly a pilgrim saint, she and her companions traveled all over Spain by donkey cart, often finding shelter in primitive hostels along the way. While facing extraordinary difficulties, Teresa never despaired of her path. She regarded her poverty as an asset rather than a handicap. "Teresa and her few ducats are indeed nothing," she once explained, "but God, Teresa, and these ducats are enough."

The sisters became known as discalced—shoeless—Carmelites. (In fact, they wore hemp sandals such as a poor person might wear.) A strict enclosure was to be maintained. What contact there was with visitors occurred through a barred grille. Their diet excluded meat. Convent life centered on prayer.

Through most of her years of public life Teresa was the target of passionate opposition from within her own Carmelite family as well as from some of the church hierarchy. Poverty is praised in the gospel but often it has been a matter of furious controversy within the church. Teresa and her writings were the object of investigation by the Spanish Inquisition. "I am really much more afraid of those who have so great a fear of the devil," she wrote in her autobiography, "than I am of the devil himself. Satan can do me no harm whatever, but they can trouble me very much." Her friend, confessor, and collaborator, the poet and mystic Saint John of the Cross, was imprisoned for nine months by his fellow monks in a dungeon of a Carmelite monastery in Toledo, during which period he was lashed at least once a week.

Few saints had such a variety of mystical experiences as Teresa. These she described in her autobiography. She also wrote several volumes on prayer. "Prayer," she said, "is nothing else than being on terms of friendship with God." Though granted experiences of mystical union that few can imagine, she never lost her ability to communicate in a very accessible way with the most ordinary people. She regarded no one with contempt. "It is love alone," she said, "that gives worth to all things."

"Remember that you have only one soul," she advised her fellow nuns. "You have only one death to die. You have only one life, which is short and has to be lived by you alone. Remember that there is only one glory, which is eternal. If you do this, there will be many things about which you care nothing."

One of her prayers has become well known in many languages: "Let nothing disturb you, nothing dismay you. All thing are passing. God never changes. Patient endurance attains all things. Whoever has God lacks nothing. God alone suffices."

Teresa died in 1582, again on a pilgrimage to launch a new foundation.

It happens from time to time that a pilgrim becomes one of those who welcomes and cares for pilgrims. Among these was a Russian peasant, Saint Matrona Popova.[21]

Few have had a harder start in life. Matrona was born in 1769 in the town of Elets in the Russian province of Orlov, nearly five hundred miles northeast of Moscow. Her father, a destitute sacristan serving the local parish, died soon after her birth. So overwhelming was the family's poverty that her mother had to give away Matrona's older sister. Matrona's mother died when Matrona was seven, leaving a paralyzed son in Matrona's care. Through odd jobs, Matrona managed to keep her brother alive for three years. Following his death, Matrona was taken in by a local family whom she served for fifteen years by caring for the children, working in the fields, washing clothes, tending animals, and assisting in the kitchen.

Having grown into a strong and able adult, she received several offers of marriage, but she never said yes to her suitors, having a vague sense that she was called to something else, though what that might be was not at all clear to her. Contact with a saintly local nun, Mother Melania, helped her find the path she was looking for. After one conversation with Mother Melania, Matrona later recalled that she had never been so happy in her life. "Melania explained to me the limitless love of God for fallen humanity. . . . This worldly life, with its mixture of earthly and deceiving impressions, which never had pleased me, now lost once and for all its attractions for me."

Matrona's immediate response was to ask if she might join a nearby convent, but Mother Melania instead suggested she go on pilgrimage, walking to Zadonsk to pray at the grave of Saint Tikhon, a bishop who had been born a peasant. He had at the time not yet been formally canonized but was widely recognized as a person who revealed Christ. (Tikhon would later be one of two models Dostoevsky drew on in creating the figure of the holy monk Father Zosima in *The Brothers Karamazov.* Tikhon was an example of the principle of active love that was at the core of Dostoevsky's writing.)

Matrona made her journey in 1794, just eleven years after Tikhon's death. Once in Zadonsk, she heard many stories of Tikhon's compassion, charity, and personal care for the poor. He became for her an exemplar of holiness.

After returning to Elets, Matrona continued to think about becoming a nun, but Mother Melania gave her unexpected advice. Return to Zadonsk, she proposed, but this time not only as a pilgrim but as someone who would care for people in need, including pilgrims, many of whom were hungry, homeless, and ill.

For Matrona, it was as if she had been asked to grow wings and fly to the moon. How could a penniless, illiterate peasant provide shelter for other poor people? "Not having anything at all, not even friends in Zadonsk, how could I care for anyone?" she asked. "I have no shelter even for myself." Mother Melania responded, "Don't doubt but believe."

Matrona returned to Zadonsk, dressed only in rags, in a town that had no place of shelter for strangers, even though the grave of Tikhon was attracting more and more pilgrims. Not knowing what else to do, she returned day by day to Tikhon's grave while at night she slept under the stars not far away.

Two of the monks of the monastery, having become aware of her seemingly endless vigil, urged a local benefactor to give Matrona use of a room. He agreed, and immediately it became a shelter not only for Matrona but for other pilgrims. This was more than the benefactor had bargained for—not many days passed before he turned Matrona and her guests out, slamming the door behind them.

The two monks persisted in their support. They raised twelve rubles, and with this sum they bought Matrona a little cabin. This now became a house of hospitality, providing room for five or six guests at a time.

The local authorities found Matrona's care of vagrants annoying and decided it was not quite legal. Matrona was arrested several times, jailed once, and even beaten, then sent back to Elets on the grounds that she had no right to be in Zadonsk because she had no internal passport.

Matrona was far from defeated. In Elets she acquired an internal passport, then returned to her hut in Zadonsk and resumed providing shelter for poor pilgrims and other wanderers.

For a time all went well. The two monks who had bought the hut continued their support, donating food and encouraging gifts from others.

But then came a great setback—her monastic helpers fell ill and died. Matrona now felt too alone in her work to continue. She set off on another pilgrimage, this time to the distant arctic island of Solovetsky in the White Sea, and from there to the Monastery of the Caves in Kiev, far to the south.

Perhaps, like so many Russians of the nineteenth century, she would have continued in a life of permanent pilgrimage had it not been for a vision that came to her while in Kiev. In a dream, Saint Barbara, one of the martyrs of the early church, urged Matrona to return to Zadonsk and resume her work of hospitality. Matrona took the dream as a message from God and obeyed.

After two more years of caring for pilgrims in her cabin, a local merchant who had been touched by Matrona's way of life offered her use of a floor in his home. With such support, the officials of the town became less irritated by her activities.

It was about this time that several unmarried women volunteered to assist her in the work she was doing, thus forming the nucleus of a community that would last more than a century, until all such communities were suppressed by the Communists.

Several years passed before Matrona had another vision. This time it was Saint Tikhon himself asking her to build "a stone house" for pilgrims and the poor. She had no idea how to undertake such a project, but almost immediately a stone mason turned up, offering his services on credit. Soon a donor arrived with a gift of two hundred rubles, a great sum at the time. Just as money was needed to provide a roof, another visitor left a handful of gold coins. Time and again, whenever money was needed, a donor would knock on the door.

No one in need was turned away, with Matrona always ready to give up her own bed if necessary. Many pilgrims spent their last days in the care of Matrona and those who assisted her, and were then buried as if they were relatives, as indeed they were regarded by the sisters.

Those who knew her saw in Matrona a person living a life of constant prayer. Sewing garments for orphans or nursing the sick, she recited the Jesus Prayer. It was, in fact, quite a structured life she followed as the years passed—certain prayers at certain times each day. Though she had become literate only late in life, she had a fine memory for prayers and knew many by heart. Among those she regularly recited was an *akathist* (a prayer of praise) for Mary:

> *My most gracious queen, my hope, Mother of God, shelter of orphans and intercessor for travelers, strangers and pilgrims, joy of those who sorrow, protectress of the wronged, see my distress, see my affliction! Help me for I am helpless. Feed me for I am a stranger and pilgrim.*

In 1851, just months before Matrona's death, she sought official recognition of the work of her community of women from the Holy Synod of the Russian Orthodox Church. The blessing was given, though it took nine years. Matrona's community was far from the usual model of monastic life, and thus not something easily blessed by the synod: a life not of quiet withdrawal to a remote location but of hospitality and nursing within a busy town, all the more busy for the magnetic pull of Saint Tikhon's relics, and, in time, of Matrona's.

Another of the great saints of pilgrimage is Benedict Joseph Labré.

During a visit to the French town where Thomas Merton was born, Prades in the eastern Pyrenees, we discovered a statue of Benedict just inside the door of the local church. He is in traditional pilgrim attire—long cloak and broad-brimmed hat with a cockle shell. He is holding a cross in one hand, pressed against his chest, a rosary in the other, and wearing boots so worn that his toes are visible.

Benedict was born of middle-class parents in a village near Boulogne, France, in 1748. While in his teens he had the longing to become a monk, but none of his several attempts at life in a monastic community was successful. It must have been a period of crushing disappointments for him. After

a breakdown of his health in 1769, while staying at the Cistercian Abbey of Sept-Fonts, a new idea began to form in his mind. He wondered if it might be God's will that, like the legendary Saint Alexis,[22] he should abandon a settled life and instead begin a life of continuous pilgrimage, walking to centers of Christian devotion.

Once his health was restored, Benedict set forward on his journey with a rosary around his neck. All that defended him from the elements was an old coat. In a bag, he carried a New Testament, a prayer book, and a copy of *The Imitation of Christ.* Like many a tramp before him, he usually slept on the ground in the open air, though in bad weather he sought shelter in barns, sheds, and pilgrim hospices. His diet was simple, mainly bread and herbs. More often than not, what he ate was either given to him or found in the garbage. He rarely begged, but there were always caring people who readily saw his need and gave him alms. Much of what he received he gave to others still poorer than he was.

It is amazing how much of the world one can see without a coin in one's pocket or the benefit of horses, cars, airplanes, trains, or ships. During the first seven years of walking, his pilgrimage brought him to many of the principal Christian shrines of western Europe–Assisi, Naples, Bari, Fabriano, and Loreto in Italy; Einsiedeln in Switzerland; Parav-le-Monial in France; and Santiago de Compostela in Spain.

Due to declining health the last six of his thirteen years of pilgrimage were lived within a smaller compass. Apart from an annual journey to Loreto, an Italian shrine linked with devotion to Christ's mother, he stayed in Rome, a city crowded with churches, shrines, and other pilgrim places, some dating back to the first century. Each day he walked to one or another place to pray. During these years he became a familiar figure to the citizens of Rome–a quiet man, one of the city's poor, and yet distinctive in the sense of deep peace he seemed to radiate. His self-denial and meekness, his unhesitating care for others, and his obvious faith and love of prayer touched many who came in contact with this destitute but untroubled man.

He never complained or exhibited distress. In his final years, rather than sleep out of doors, he took shelter in one of Rome's hospices for the poor. Nevertheless, the years of deprivation took their toll and his health gave out. On April 16, 1783, Benedict Joseph Labré collapsed on the steps of the church of Santa Maria dei Monti and was carried to the neighboring house of a butcher, where he died.

Devotion to Benedict quickly took root, first of all from children who carried the news about the city, shouting, "The saint is dead!" A century later this unwashed and flea-bitten man in rags, who had tried and failed to become a monk, was canonized and declared a patron saint of pilgrims.

The death of saints seems only to make them more present among the living. It is not simply that their memory is persistent, but that they become a leaven in many other lives.

Their pilgrimage becomes intertwined with the pilgrimages of others. Once formally recognized as saints and placed on the church calendar, their icons and statues are bathed in the light of thousands of candles. In prayer, faithful people appeal for their intercession. Their stories evolve into legends. They walk at our side, part of a "cloud of witnesses," as the Letter to the Hebrews puts it. So long as they are not presented in superhuman terms by hagiographers, they help us understand more fully what it means to be human, and what we ourselves might be capable of.

If saints are only a special breed of people with an extra bit of halo-producing DNA, what good are they? Such a superhuman species would only make the rest of us feel inadequate. But, in fact, saints are flawed people, like ourselves, whose lives, when shown warts and all, always bear the message, "If I can do it, anyone can."

No saint regards himself or herself as worthy of a halo. Dorothy Day said, "Don't call me a saint—I don't want to be dismissed that easily." But she saw sanctity as everyone's vocation. On the front page of the newspaper she edited, she once made a banner headline of Saint Paul's words, "We are all called to be saints."

Thin Places

We think that Paradise and Calvary,
Christ's Cross and Adam's Tree, stood in one place;
Look Lord and find both Adams met in me;
As the first Adam's sweat surrounds my face,
May the last Adam's blood my soul embrace.

–JOHN DONNE,
"HYMN TO GOD, MY GOD, IN MY SICKNESS"

The question our century puts before us is: is it possible
to regain the lost dimension, the encounter with the Holy,
the dimension which cuts through the world of subjec-
tivity and objectivity and goes down to that which is not
world but is the Mystery of the Ground of Being?

–PAUL TILLICH

Life is this simple. We are living in a world that is
absolutely transparent and God is shining through all
the time. This is not just a fable or a nice story. It is
true. If we abandon ourselves to God and forget ourselves, we see it sometimes, and we see it maybe frequently. God shows himself everywhere, in everything—
in people and in things and in nature and in events. It
becomes very obvious that God is everywhere and in everything and we cannot be without him. It's impossible.
The only thing is that we don't see it.

–THOMAS MERTON,
"LIFE AND SOLITUDE" (TAPES)

*P*ilgrimage is the quest for what the Celts have described as thin places. Thin places have a way of slowing us down, even stopping us in our tracks.

A thin place is one where ordinary matter seems charged with God's presence. It may be a spot widely known for a celebrated encounter with God, a place remembered for a key event in the life of Jesus, or a place linked with a great saint; it may be twelve time zones away, close at hand, or right where you are standing. What marks any thin place is the time-stopping awareness of God's presence. It doesn't matter whether a particular thin place is known only to you or featured in hundreds of guidebooks. For you, that spot will be endowed ever after with a special significance.

Thin places, even when built of stone, seem to possess a kind of translucence. While awareness of the Divine Presence—in reality, everywhere—is forced upon no one, in a thin place an awareness of the holy often touches even the most skeptical and faith-resistant person. The walls of ancient churches seem to have been sponge-like in absorbing the prayers and tears of all who have come there. All that makes life opaque has slowly been worn away by so many pilgrims bringing their suffering, their longing, their prayers, their grief, their gratitude, their joy.

The most famous thin places are powerful magnets attracting pilgrims by the thousands or even millions. They come by foot and bike, car and bus, plane and train; they come alone, and they come in crowds.

An encyclopedia of many volumes could be written describing all the world's thin places. But for the moment let us consider only three.

One of the most venerable of thin places is Mount Sinai and its surroundings. Moses got there on foot. Most pilgrims these days arrive by bus.

About thirteen hundred years before Christ's birth, Moses murdered an Egyptian who was abusing a Hebrew. Desperately in need of a hiding place, he fled to the southern Sinai, a desert region of narrow valleys and precipitous cliffs. There, years later, beside a well, he met his wife, Zipporah. While guarding his father-in-law's flock near the same well, he experienced the miracle of the burning bush. Before his eyes a desert bush exploded with flame yet wasn't consumed. From within the burning bush God called, "Moses, Moses!" Moses replied, "Here I am." The voice spoke again: "Come no closer. Remove the sandals from your feet, for the place on which you are standing is holy ground." Finally the voice identified itself: "I am the God of your father, the God of Abraham, the God of Isaac, and the God of Jacob." The text in Exodus continues, "And Moses hid his face, for he was afraid to look at God" (Ex 3:4–6). On that day Moses found the next step in his vocation: to return to Egypt and free his fellow Jews from slavery.

While the bush Moses stood before no longer burns, it lived a long life. Its progeny has survived to the present day. In the year 330 the Byzantine empress, Helena, requested the monks living in the area to build a chapel next to the site of the bush. Later in the same century the Spanish nun Egeria was among pilgrims who came here. "There are many cells of holy men," she wrote, "and a church on the spot where the bush stands, and this bush is still alive today and gives forth shoots." The bush, quite large, still thrives within an enclosure adjacent to a chapel directly behind the basilica's main sanctuary.

In the sixth century substantial donations from the Emperor Justinian made possible construction of a basilica and the fortress wall that still encloses the monastery. Even with this formidable barrier, however, the monks could do little in self-defense under siege. One of the wonders of the Christian era is that this vulnerable desert community has survived. Its principal defense is not its granite walls, but a document signed by the prophet Muhammad personally guaranteeing the safety of the monastery and its inhabitants. It is one of the principal treasures of the monastery library. For centuries, Muslim Bedouin neighbors, who venerate Moses and Mary and regard Jesus as a prophet, have assisted the monks. As an act of gratitude and hospitality to its guardians, St. Catherine's is the world's only monastery to have a mosque within its walls.

The monastery opens its gate to visitors only three hours a day, between nine and noon.[23] Praying at the place of the burning bush may be the pilgrims' first priority, but they find much more to do both within the walls of St. Catherine's and in the surrounding wilderness.

First of all, there is the iconography. The monks care for some of the world's oldest and finest icons. Two hundred of them hang in a special gallery. Among the earliest is an image of the face of Christ that has a photographic immediacy. A sixth-century icon of Saint Peter is so lifelike that, if smaller, it could be used in a passport. That these icons have survived is thanks to the irony of the monastery's being situated in the Muslim world and thus beyond the edicts of the iconoclastic Byzantine emperors of the eighth and ninth centuries.

Among the monastery's less ancient icons is one from the thirteenth century that shows Moses taking off his sandals before the burning bush.

Outside the walls Mount Sinai towers over the monastery. As it rises, it divides into three peaks, the most famous being Jebel Musa, the Peak of Moses. Mount Sinai seems not just to have risen but to have erupted out of the earth. It is as barren a place as exists anywhere on earth.

Moses climbed the mountain on two occasions to speak with God. Regarding the second ascent, Exodus records:

> Then Moses went up on the mountain, and the cloud covered the mountain. The glory of the LORD settled on Mount Sinai, and the cloud covered it six days; on the seventh day he called to Moses out of the midst of the cloud. Now the appearance of the glory of the LORD was like a devouring fire on the top of the mountain in the sight of the people of Israel. Moses entered the cloud, and went up on the mountain. Moses was on the mountain forty days and forty nights. (Ex 24:15–18)

During those forty days Moses received the two tablets on which the Ten Commandments were inscribed.

In the first millennium, monks living on and near Mount Sinai created a 3,750–step granite stairway that makes the ascent for today's pilgrims much easier than it was for Moses.[24] Pilgrims normally start the climb in the middle of the night so they can witness the sunrise from the summit. The small church on the top, on the spot where Moses talked with God and received the Ten Commandments, is about sixteen hundred years old.

Few places on earth are less favorable to human presence than Mount Sinai and the surrounding area, yet countless thousands of monks have made this desert region, including the mountain heights, their home for more than seventeen centuries. At the same time, they have received and cared for a never-ending river of pilgrims.

No matter how brief the visit, no pilgrim can leave St. Catherine's without being impressed with the fierce tenacity of monastic life in such a dry, rugged, sun-battered setting. One need only read any of the collections of desert-father stories to meet some of the astonishing people who have made the Egyptian desert their home.[25]

The best known monk of St. Catherine's Monastery was Saint John Climacus (or Saint John of the Ladder), abbot of the monastery for many years until his death in the year 606, when he was in his eighties. He is the author of one of the classics of ascetic life, *The Ladder of Divine Ascent*. This is the only book that has its own icon, an image that with great economy summarizes the text: A thirty-rung ladder links the desert to the welcoming hands of Christ in heaven, but many are falling from it. The book is a kind of guidebook outlining the route to salvation for monks to follow. A ladder of thirty virtues begins with the renunciation of worldly life and ascends, rung by rung, through obedience, penitence, detachment, and humility to enter into love of God and of neighbor and freedom from all that impedes that love. The book's moral isn't how easy it is to fall, but rather how important it is to get up and start climbing again after each fall. This is what generations of monks at St. Catherine's have been struggling to do.

While St. Catherine's is among the most honored and impressive places of Christian pilgrimage anywhere on earth, the oldest and most important pilgrimage center for Christians is Jerusalem. Despite all its sorrows, Jerusalem remains a city crowded with thin places, chief of which is the Church of the Resurrection, as it is called by Orthodox Christians, or the Church of the Holy Sepulcher, as it is known to Christians of other traditions.

As is often the case with much-visited thin places, pilgrims frequently find themselves unready once they arrive, no matter how much preparation they have made. Standing at the door of the church, many pilgrims are in a state of exhaustion and irritation rather than astonishment and exaltation. They have endured the wear and tear of simply arriving only to meet the obstacle of slow-moving lines once inside the church. Many pilgrims find themselves struggling to calm their frayed nerves as they attempt to focus their thoughts on what happened there two millennia ago. After all this hard work, the pilgrim may not be in a receptive state. On top of that, there may be the disappointment of what time has done to such a place. Nothing inside the church looks anything as it did twenty centuries ago.

For most pilgrims stepping into that dimly lit, time-worn church, the first stop is the chapel on Golgotha, where Jesus gave up his life on the cross.

The chapel, reached by ascending a narrow stone staircase just inside the main entrance, is dominated by a life-sized icon of Christ on the cross, in front of which is a marble altar standing on four thin pillars. Dozens of candles burn constantly, while numerous ornate silver lamps, large and small, hang from the ceiling. Glass panels on either side of the altar reveal the rough stone surface on which the cross was erected outside the city walls, which stood nearby in the days of Roman occupation. (Following the city's destruction in AD 70, Jerusalem was rebuilt within new walls, at which time the western wall was moved further west, enclosing Golgotha.)

Cluttered as it is with pre-Reformation religious imagery, this chapel can be a disorienting place for Protestant visitors. They may also be disconcerted to witness the physical veneration exhibited by pilgrims belonging to the older churches. Yet once inside the chapel, the most undemonstrative visitor tends to be moved by the climate of quiet, heartfelt devotion shown by pilgrims from the more ancient traditions. Even a tourist with a head full of religious doubts may feel obliged to speak in a whisper. Visitors who regard the resurrection as nothing more than a pious legend may be moved by the realization that here, on this very spot, a man who had harmed no one—a man of mercy and healing—was stripped, nailed to a cross, and left to die while soldiers threw dice to determine who would take possession of his bloodstained robe. Nearly all visitors kneel in front of the altar, then reach through an opening in the marble floor to touch the rock of Golgotha.

Another significant resonance for this place is the tradition that Adam and Eve were buried at Golgotha, the very place where Christ was later crucified. In any icon of the Byzantine tradition, Adam's skull appears in a tiny black cave just under the foot of the cross.[26]

Leaving the Golgotha chapel, most pilgrims stop at the place where, according to Christian memory, Christ's body was laid out before burial. The stone tablet set into the floor, placed there many centuries ago and now as smooth as silk, has received not only millions of kisses but also a river of tears and a nearly constant flow of perfume, the latter poured mainly by women pilgrims. Each day brings many hundreds of mourners who pause at this small area just inside the church's main entrance. The pilgrims among them know the significance of this rectangle of stone on which no one steps, while tourists are mainly puzzled and perhaps embarrassed by the intense emotion they see displayed by the people kneeling there.

The next stop for pilgrim and tourist alike is the tomb in which Christ rose from the dead. It is about 100 feet west of the Golgotha chapel and directly beneath the church's main dome.

When Jesus was crucified, this was the Garden of Golgotha, full of olive trees and flowering plants. What was once a small and ordinary burial place—a simple niche chiseled out of a stone embankment, one among many—has become an elaborately carved, chapel-like structure. The surrounding embankment and the adjacent tombs have been completely cut away since the fourth century.

To accommodate pilgrims, Christ's tomb has been made larger than it was. The structure encasing the tomb—called the Aedicula—now has within it both an outer and inner room, the latter with the narrow shelf, now covered with a thin sheet of marble, on which Christ's body was laid.

Worn nerves and aching feet notwithstanding, pilgrims always find it a blessing to enter this constricted enclosure. At the very least, the gospel accounts of the mystery of Christ's triumph over death become more real. It probably crosses even the atheist visitor's mind that what occurred here may not be merely an ancient fable. Something happened in this small space that every subsequent generation has had to consider—a mysterious event that has shifted culture and history and even altered the way we look at one another. The place of the resurrection continuously attracts people from near and far, touches both intellect and heart, and provides a summons to live the rest of one's life in the freedom that comes from no longer dreading death.

The Church of the Resurrection is more than an enclosure for two sacred places. The pilgrim who has time will discover many unexpected surprises by wandering alone through this maze-like church.

One of my most memorable experiences inside this ancient church occurred during Easter in 1985. How fortunate I was! It is all but impossible to get inside the church on Pascha. One must have an invitation. Providentially, George Hintlian, a leader of Jerusalem's Armenian Christian community, had given me one. It was a precious gift. Each of the several Christian communities in Jerusalem is allotted only so many. Once the guests are inside the church, the doors are locked and bolted. The area immediately around the tomb is densely crowded.

At a certain moment the patriarch of Jerusalem, having entered the tomb and been locked inside, lights the "holy fire." Flame bursts out of the tomb's small windows. The sealed doors are opened, and the patriarch comes out bearing two candles, which are then used to light the candles everyone holds. Few people hold only one; more often each holds ten or twelve. Each candle will later become a gift to a friend or relative who couldn't be present. Meanwhile, guests utter cries of joy not unlike those one might hear in a crowded sports stadium at the moment a winning point is scored in a crucial game. As at a sports match, some exultant young men ride on the shoulders of friends. It is an amazing sight. The space around the tomb quickly becomes hot from the proximity of so many people. So many living flames—so many people packed so tightly! Those who suffer from claustrophobia may find it slightly terrifying.

During the hours when we were locked inside the church, I twice retreated from the crowd to empty areas away from the tomb.

First I went back to Golgotha. How strange it is to be at a place normally crowded with pilgrims and to be the only one there. It is a rare blessing to be entirely alone at the exact spot where Christ gave himself for the life of the world.

On my second walk away from the tumult surrounding the tomb, I went as far as the east end of the church. Walking down the stairway to Saint Helena's Chapel and from there to another, deeper level, I entered the Chapel of the Discovery of the Cross.

While all visitors to the church visit the place of the crucifixion and the tomb in which Christ's body was laid, far fewer visit this remote corner. Many visitors don't have time. People often travel long and far to reach Jerusalem, and then face a tight schedule once they arrive. As a result, they see relatively little of this huge, somewhat chaotic, ancient building with its many passageways, staircases, chapels, and places of veneration. In fact, many Protestant tour groups, suspicious of relics and uncomfortable with devotion to saints, intentionally avoid this subterranean chapel. "The true cross? Found here?" one may hear a visitor say. "Hogwash! All these so-called relics! It was a hoax—just some old wood in the ground passed off as the real thing by swindlers."

The pilgrim descends a stone staircase. Step by step the air gets cooler and damper. He or she goes slowly, perhaps pausing to notice the carefully carved graffiti on the walls left by the pilgrims of earlier eras. Finally, the pilgrim reaches an exceptionally quiet, womb-like area beneath the huge church.

There is something remarkable about the special quietness of this deep, damp chapel. Even when there is a steady stream of people coming and going, it seems to absorb and muffle every sound. The unhurried visitor can feel a numinous quality here that may be harder to experience in places where people are waiting in slow-moving lines. In a subterranean enclosure entirely abandoned at Easter, I found myself more aware of the risen Christ than when I stood outside his tomb. An ancient garbage pit has become the thinnest of thin places.

I was also aware of being in the footsteps of Saint Helena, whose pilgrim journey in the year 326 inspired the discovery of the cross. Twenty years later, Saint Cyril, bishop of Jerusalem, declared, "[The Cross] has been distributed fragment by fragment from this spot and already has nearly filled all the world."

Another thin place, goal of many pilgrims despite its size and remoteness, is the tiny island of Iona in Scotland's Inner Hebrides. This comma of land just off the southwest tip of Mull has been a place of pilgrimage for nearly fifteen hundred years.

In the course of walking Iona's paths, you will find yourself standing on some of the oldest exposed rock on earth.

The more imposing volcanic heights of neighboring Mull belong to a land just barely out of the baby carriage in comparison—a mere seventy million years old. Iona is vastly older: two-and-a-half billion years.

An Irish saint, Columba, put Iona on the map. In penance for his role in a bloody clan war, Columba, along with twelve companions, sailed away from his homeland in self-exile, arriving on Iona on Pentecost Sunday in the year 563. Walking across the island from what has since been known as Columba's Bay, his group found an ideal spot to build a monastic settlement on the northeast edge of the island.

Iona is the probable birthplace of the greatest masterpiece of Celtic art, the illuminated gospel text known as the Book of Kells. The book takes its name from a monastery in Ireland where it was later taken for safekeeping. It is now displayed in the library of Trinity College, Dublin.

The wattle-and-daub dwellings the monks lived in fifteen centuries ago are long gone, destroyed by Viking raids between 795 and 806. During those years sixty-seven of the monks were martyred. At last, the survivors packed up and returned to Ireland. All that remains from the early days of monastic life on Iona are several standing crosses, the tiny chapel of Saint Oran, the adjacent graveyard in which many kings and queens of ancient Ireland and Scotland are buried, Macbeth among them, and the faint traces of foundations.

What today's pilgrims find are the solid stone buildings Benedictine monks erected in the thirteenth century, when monastic life found fresh footing on Iona: the plain square tower of St. Mary's Cathedral and the rectangular masses of the several adjoining buildings are all of enduring gray stone with deep-cut windows under steep, slated roofs.

The monks of Columba's day lived a demanding life spent close to the elements. Columba's monastic rule, later adopted by many similar communities, required that the monks own nothing but bare necessities, inhabit a place with but one door, center their conversations on God and the New Testament, refuse idle words and the spreading of rumor and evil reports, and follow every rule that governs devotion. They were to prepare themselves daily for suffering and death, to offer forgiveness from the heart to everyone, to put almsgiving before all other duties, and to eat nothing unless hungry; they were not to sleep unless tired; they were to pray constantly for anyone who had trouble, and to pray until tears came. They were to labor to the point of tears as well, or, if tears "are not free, until thy perspiration come often."

Columban monastic life was far from sedentary. The monks of Iona traveled into the wilds of Scotland and, later on, much further as missionaries of the gospel. They also served as a pacifying influence in a Europe of small kingdoms and constant war. Irish monasticism had a profound impact on the development both of Christianity and culture across Europe, even reaching to France, Italy, and western Russia. Missionaries sent from Iona founded schools and communities, winning in the process such a reputation for holiness that, even in the sixth century, pilgrims were drawn to the remote isle from as far away as Rome. Tiny Iona became known as the Jerusalem of the North.

Much of the thirty-two years of life left to Columba once he arrived on Iona were spent preaching the Christian faith to the unchurched inhabitants of the highlands of northern Scotland. His preaching was confirmed by many miracles. He provided for the nurturing of his converts by building many churches and monasteries. He governed numerous communities in Ireland and Scotland, which recognized him as spiritual father and founder. When not away on missionary travels, Columba resided on Iona.

Witnesses record that Columba never spent a waking hour without study, prayer, or useful work. A lover of books from his early years, he was often engaged in the work of transcription. Reportedly, he copied more than three hundred books with his own hand. Two of these, *The Book of Durrow* and the psalter called *The Cathach*, survive to the present day.

One of the most revealing of the many stories that come down to us about Columba's life concerns a sword. It was the custom of people who visited him not only to seek a blessing for themselves, but also for some item of personal property. One day, without due reflection, Columba blessed a sword that was put before him, only to realize afterward that it might well be used in battle. He then gave the sword

a second, more careful blessing, praying that the blade would remain sharp only so long as it was used for cutting bread and cheese but would acquire a dull edge if ever used to harm any living thing.

The medieval abbey seems as timeless as the island's seagulls. So solid and undamaged does the monastery appear that it is startling to see old engravings showing the ruined state it fell into after the Scottish Parliament outlawed monastic life in 1561. The Act of Suppression came just two years before the thousand-year anniversary of the first monks landing on Iona. It was only in the last century that restoration at last occurred, thanks mainly to the efforts of a Presbyterian minister, George MacLeod, pastor of a working-class parish in Glasgow. Inspired by MacLeod, pilgrims came to Iona not simply to admire the ruins and try to imagine what had once happened there, but to take part in the hard physical labor of restoration. The restored abbey in turn has greatly enlarged the number of pilgrims coming to Iona.[27]

No doubt Saint Columba rejoices to see Iona's revival as a place of Christian life and a center of pilgrimage, one of the world's thin places. He had a gift for seeing the future and knew one day there would be nothing left of his foundation, but he saw beyond that desolate time to its restoration. He left this prophecy:

> *Iona of my heart,*
> *Iona of my love,*
> *Instead of monk's voices,*
> *Shall be lowing of cattle,*
> *But ere the world comes to an end*
> *Iona shall be as it was.*

Dark Places,
Dark Paths

If you wish to be sure of the road you are traveling, close your eyes and walk in the dark.

—SAINT JOHN OF THE CROSS

Pilgrimage happens when you're not moving. You learn when you're unlearning. Revelation comes in gulps that leave you gasping, but sometimes it seems to come in the slow accumulation of small insights that you hardly know have happened, in chance encounters and odd surprises, in little glimpses of what you did not go to see and did not know was there.

—PAUL CHANDLER

If thin places are focal points of pilgrimage where ordinary matter seems to shine with God's presence, perhaps we can describe those places that seem forever shadowed with the power of destruction as dark places—battlefields, places of torture or mass execution, areas associated with genocide, slave markets, and concentration camps—all those places that seem at first to proclaim the absence of God. For Christian pilgrims, such places offer a dark path, as it has been called by such mystics as Saint John of the Cross. The dark path is the way of namelessness and unknowing—the way of the cross. Just as the cross is linked to the resurrection, so dark paths can lead the pilgrim to heaven. The thinnest of all thin places, the Jerusalem church built over the place of Christ's resurrection, in fact stands over what at first seemed to Christ's followers the darkest of dark places.

I live a short walk from a dark place: the former synagogue of the Dutch city of Alkmaar. It's a brick building with a roof of orange tiles. There is a wide door in the center and just above it a circular window. Whenever taking guests on a walk through the town, I try to include the building on whatever route we take, translating for the visitor the words on the plaque to the left of the building's main entrance:

> The house of the explorer and cartographer Cornelis Drebbel (1572–1633) stood in this place. On June 5, 1808, the property was purchased by the Jewish congregation for the purpose of establishing a synagogue. In 1842, to the rear of the synagogue, a school was founded for religious and civil studies; the classes were taught by the rabbi, who lived next door to the synagogue at number 13. Two decorative stones with Hebrew texts were placed in the facade, the first in 1826 and the other in 1844. The house was given a neoclassical facade, barrel vaulting with a star of David, a women's gallery, and an extension in the back for the Ark in which the Torah scrolls were stored. On March 5, 1942, 213 Jews were transported to Amsterdam and the interior of the synagogue was plundered. Only a few returned.

I always find it difficult to read the last two sentences, becoming speechless with grief. On that ordinary March day, the scent of spring in the air, normal life ended for all the Jews in this small city. Police, armed with maps in which each Alkmaar house occupied by Jews was marked in red, brought the arrested families to the synagogue—grandparents, young couples, teens, children, infants. That same day they were taken to a theater in the Jewish district of Amsterdam for initial processing, then sent to the one Dutch concentration camp, Westerbork. From there they were transported to various concentration camps in Germany and occupied Poland. The majority went to Auschwitz. Few survived.

I can imagine the dread in their faces as they arrived at the synagogue, their sense of absolute powerlessness, their vague awareness that the journey that was beginning that day would never bring them home again. Children would not have been the only ones crying.

Many of their neighbors who watched them being taken away did so without even waving goodbye. Indeed, many Dutch people in various ways collaborated in the removal of the Jews from the Netherlands. There were all those people who filled in forms, made arrests, transported those arrested, or played other small roles in the complex machinery of the Holocaust–and far more who passively watched it all happen–as well as all those who might have extended a helping hand but failed to.

For nearly five hundred years, since the Jewish expulsion from Spain in 1492, Alkmaar had been a place of welcome and security for Jews. But after the Nazi occupation of Holland began in May 1940, Jews in Alkmaar, as in other Dutch towns and cities, quickly found themselves subject to more and more restrictions. They were obliged to wear a yellow star, excluded from theaters, permitted to shop only at prescribed times, forbidden to own bicycles or use trams, required to be home from 8 p.m. to 6 a.m., barred from the civil service, stripped of respected posts, and prohibited from visiting Christians in their homes, all the while being made the object of grossly dehumanizing propaganda. One short film screened in Dutch cinemas in those days showed the transformation of a Jewish face into the face of a rat.

The most resourceful and lucky ones managed to find hiding places. The Dutch underground hid a large number of Jews, between 25,000 and 30,000, many of whom survived. But approximately 110,000 Jews were rounded up and deported from the Netherlands. Between 1940 and 1945, more than 75 percent of the Dutch Jewish population died, many killed outright, others by malnutrition, exposure, and disease. Only 5,200 Dutch Jews who had been sent to Nazi concentration camps survived.

Whenever I stand outside Alkmaar's former synagogue, I find I am making a pilgrimage into my own dark side. It seems to me what happened there occurred days ago rather than decades, and that, had I lived here then, I might have been among those who assisted in the roundup. To be a Nazi, or just to be someone who helps Nazis with their dirty work, requires no odd variety of DNA that makes the commission of evil actions more likely. The potential is in me, and in each of us. All those who created and assisted the Holocaust and other acts of mass persecution and murder were ordinary people whose ideas, attitudes, and actions had been distorted by propaganda and prejudice or who were simply too afraid, or too driven by the will to survive, to disobey.

Well over half a century has passed. Germans these days come to Holland not as occupiers but to enjoy its museums and North Sea beaches. Especially in the summertime, we hear many German voices. The Germans are made welcome by most Dutch people, and yet the shadow left by the years of occupation still darkens the Dutch soul.

The most visited dark place in the Netherlands is an inconspicuous four-storey building on the Prinsengracht in Amsterdam. Even on a cold and rainy day there is always a line of people waiting to enter the Anne Frank House. Nearly a million visitors (a good many of them German) pass through its entrance each year.

What draws so many people to this address is chiefly the memory of a gifted young writer who lived in hiding at this address and finally died in a concentration camp. But the house on the Prinsengracht is not only a memorial to one victim of the Nazi era or even a place of connection with all victims of the Holocaust. The Anne Frank House has become a center of awareness regarding all those who are suffering persecution in our own time because of their nationality, religious tradition, or minority status.

Going into hiding was a nightmarish choice, but Anne's father, Otto Frank, could see no alternative. By the spring of 1942 Dutch Jews were already being rounded up. The Frank family had no illusions about what the Nazis intended. They had escaped from Germany to Holland in 1934, shortly after Hitler was elected chancellor. Now Holland was occupied and its borders closed. There was no exit to a safer country. Their only chance was to live out of sight.

Their hiding place was a small building—two floors, with two rooms per floor, plus a tiny attic—just behind Otto Frank's business. "The annex is an ideal place to hide in," Anne optimistically wrote in her diary. "It may be damp and lopsided, but there's probably not a more comfortable hiding place in all of Amsterdam. No, in all of Holland."

In July 1942 the Frank family moved into these tight quarters. They were joined by several friends also desperately seeking a place of refuge: first, Otto Frank's business friend, Hermann van Pels, with his wife, Auguste, and their son, Peter; and later Fritz Pfeffer, a dentist. All together they were eight. The youngest was Anne, just thirteen. She had to share her small room with Fritz Pfeffer.

The lifeline of those in hiding was a small circle of trusted non-Jewish friends and colleagues in the office: Miep and Jan Gies, Victor Kugler, Johannes Kleiman, and Bep Voskuijl. They managed to buy supplies and food (strictly rationed at the time), bring books and magazines, and take care of all other needs that arose.

The eight people in hiding had not only to remain unseen by the community beyond their heavily curtained windows but also to remain unheard. To survive, they had to live invisibly and in silence.

It was hardest during the daytime. The residents of the secret annex had to keep as quiet as mice for fear that people working in the warehouse might become aware of their presence. Their one toilet could be flushed only after hours. Living in such close quarters with no privacy was also a trial; Anne wasn't the only one who sometimes found the people with whom she lived profoundly irritating. "My mind boggles at the profanity this honorable house has had to endure in

Behind this bookcase is the entrance to the secret annex where Anne Frank and her family hid from the Nazis

the past month," she wrote in her diary. "To tell you the truth, I sometimes forget who we're at odds with and who we're not. The only way to take my mind off it is to study, and I've been doing a lot of that lately."

Of all times in life to endure a caged life, surely adolescence is the hardest: day after day in a place with no exit, elbow to elbow with one's parents, an older sister, and several others, including a boy only a few years her senior. Part of her way of coping was the deeply confessional relationship Anne developed with her diary. Besides providing a day-by-day narrative of events as they happened, she wrote about her relations with each person sharing the annex, vividly—sometimes mercilessly—describing each of them. She recorded her feelings, beliefs, frustrations, attractions, and hopes for the future, even writing about such topics as her belief in God and her views on human nature. The best thing about her diary, Anne wrote, "is being able to write down all my thoughts and feelings, otherwise I'd absolutely suffocate."

One would not blame a young woman in hiding in the Nazi era if she were to adopt a bleak view of the human race. Yet it was in the secret annex that on July 15, 1944, Anne wrote the astonishing words: "It's a wonder I haven't abandoned all my ideals, they seem so absurd and impractical. Yet I cling to them because I still believe, in spite of everything, that people are truly good at heart." By then she had been in hiding the better part of three years.

Initially her diary was a strictly private endeavor. No one in the secret annex was ever permitted to read it. But in the spring of 1944 Anne heard a radio broadcast by Gerrit Bolkestein, a member of the London-based Dutch government-in-exile. Bolkestein proposed that, when the war ended, a public archive of the Dutch people's oppression under German occupation should be created. He also looked forward to the eventual publication of letters and diaries. Thinking that her own diary might be suitable for postwar publication, Anne began editing her writing, removing some sections and rewriting others.

By the summer of 1944 it was obvious that Germany was being beaten on all fronts. Allied forces were steadily advancing. Paris had been liberated. People in hiding could begin to imagine that freedom was not far away. But in Holland the Nazi occupation was far from over. The southern area of the Netherlands was not liberated until the fall of 1944, while the northern part of the country, including Amsterdam, was not freed until May 5, 1945.

On August 4, 1944, eight months before the surrender of German forces in Holland, the occupants of the secret annex were arrested, betrayed by a person whose identity has never been discovered.

The final entry in Anne's diary was written on August 1, 1944. She was fifteen years old.

After several weeks at the Westerbork camp, the Frank family traveled by cattle car to Auschwitz. From there, Anne and her sister, Margo, were sent to Bergen-Belsen. Malnourished and ill with typhus, both died in March 1945, about eight weeks before the war in Europe ended. Their mother, Edith, had died in January.

Of the eight who had lived in the secret annex, only Otto Frank survived. Returning to Amsterdam after the war, his friend and co-worker Miep Gies gave Otto the diaries and notebooks Anne had written. She had found them scattered on the floor of the annex following the arrest.

The survival of Anne's diary seemed a miracle to Otto. "It took me a very long time before I could read it," he recalled later on. "And I must say, I was very much surprised about the deep thoughts that Anne had, her seriousness, especially her self-criticism. It was quite a different Anne than I had known as my daughter. She never really showed this kind of inner feeling. She talked about many things, criticized many things, but what her real feelings were, that I could only see from the diary."

Otto decided that the diary should be published and devoted himself to transcribing the text. Not revising anything Anne wrote, he simply removed passages that he found too harsh or too private. He didn't want to include Anne's sharp words about her mother or details about Anne's sexual maturation. In 1947 the Dutch edition was published. Soon thereafter translations began to appear in other countries. The book became an international bestseller. A play and then a film inspired by the diary were seen by millions of people. In response to the growing interest in Anne's diary, in 1960 the building on the Prinsengracht became a museum. The unabridged text of Anne's diary was published in 1995. A major expansion to the Amsterdam museum was made in 1998 to enlarge the exhibition area and accommodate the ever-growing number of visitors. The Anne Frank House also created a traveling exhibition that has been seen in hundreds of cities around the world. Now, thanks to the Internet, there is yet another point of access for anyone with a web browser.[28]

Virtual visits on computer screens are fine, but there is nothing like experiencing the actual place. Those making a pilgrimage to the Anne Frank House enter a no-frills building that would attract no special interest had it not been for Anne's diary. The building stands along one of Amsterdam's picturesque canals but is itself certainly no beauty, nor did those in hiding have rooms with a view. Once in the secret annex, to the building's rear, the canal was never seen. A block to the south there is the crown-topped tower of the Westerkerk, whose bells meant so much to Anne. It could be glimpsed through a small window in the attic.

Waiting in line to enter, one can see many signs of the modern world, but once inside the building the visitor steps back in time. Otto Frank's two businesses have been recreated:

Opekta, which sold the pectin housewives needed for making jellies and jams; and Pectacon, which manufactured a spice and herb mixture for making sausage. Otto's office is again as it was before he went into hiding. The secret annex itself is preserved as it was after the arrest of the occupants, when a Dutch company hired by the Germans stripped the annex of all its furniture. Just before entering the annex, a short film gives the visitor an idea of how the annex looked when it was in use as a hiding place. Elsewhere in the museum there is a photo display about the Frank family and those who hid with them, then an exhibition documents the rise of the Nazi movement, World War II, the Holocaust, and contemporary Nazi-like movements.

The annex had two main rooms. On the first floor, behind the hinged bookcase that was the only entrance to the annex, was the Frank family room, used at night as a bedroom for Otto, Edith, and Margo. On the floor above was the van Pels' family room. On each floor was a smaller room. Peter van Pels used the one above, and Anne and the dentist, Fritz Pfeffer, the one below.

The most memorable room, of course, is the one in which Anne Frank slept, wrote her diary, and studied. Its walls still bear traces of Anne's presence. "Our little room looked very bare at first with nothing on the walls," she wrote in her diary the same month the family went into hiding, "but thanks to Daddy who had brought my film-star collection and picture postcards beforehand, and with the aid of a paste pot and brush, I have transformed the walls into one gigantic picture. This makes it look much more cheerful." Though now covered by a protective sheet of clear plastic, the pictures of movie stars are still there, along with several postcards and photos of the younger members of the Dutch and British royal families.

My most important experience of that tiny room is vicarious. Because Nancy has done a great deal of translation work for the Anne Frank House, we have come to know many members of the staff. When one of them discovered that our daughter, Anne, was named after Anne Frank and that, inspired by her, our daughter also kept a diary, he suggested that some evening we come down after the museum had closed so that Anne might be able to spend some time alone in Anne Frank's room. Our Anne—not much younger than her namesake when she went into hiding—eagerly accepted the invitation. Once in the room, she was slow to leave. Her time in solitude there deepened an already-existing bond. Perhaps it was our Anne's first conscious experience of being a pilgrim.

Afterward, Nancy and I had a turn in the same room, studying the pictures that Anne Frank had glued to the wall and looking out the window at a huge chestnut tree that is sometimes mentioned in the diary. We said nothing. It's not a place for talk. It's a place to pray for all the people in hiding in the world today. There are so many Anne Franks.

The exhibition at the Anne Frank House reviews the events of the Nazi era, but it doesn't stop with the end of World War II. Much attention is given to the many racial, national, and religious prejudices that thrive in our time. No one can visit the Anne Frank House without becoming more conscious of the millions of people living in grave danger today.

For any visitor, the Anne Frank House raises burning questions. What would I do if I lived in a country under military occupation? How successful would I be in not having my thoughts and actions shaped by intimidation, fear, and propaganda? How would I respond to harassment, arrest, and deportation? What would I say if a friend or neighbor in danger pleaded for my help? Might fear play so decisive a role in my life that I would say, "I'm sorry, but there is nothing I can do"? Far from helping the hunted, might I even be one of those who decide that helping the hunters is a prudent and even profitable thing to do? But the most urgent questions raised by a visit to the Anne Frank House are not about what I might have done had I lived in Holland when it was an occupied country. Rather, they are these: What am I doing about endangered people in the world right now? Does the pilgrimage I am making bring me closer to such people?

No matter where you go, there are dark places close at hand.

I think of a recent visit to Memphis, Tennessee. A friend there, Therese Cullen, was in the process of opening a house of hospitality for families in need, a place of welcome appropriately named after Dorothy Day.[29] Therese had arranged for me to give a lecture about Dorothy at the city's Catholic cathedral.

While in Memphis, Therese took me on pilgrimage to several of the city's dark places.

The first was the Lorraine Motel, where Dr. Martin Luther King, Jr., was assassinated on April 4, 1968. The bloodstains on the balcony where he was shot were washed away long ago, yet Dr. King seems to remain in Memphis as an unseen presence. In recent years the motel has become the National Civil Rights Museum. Devoted to the memory of Dr. King, it also provides a history of slavery and the emergence of movements that have regarded racism and slavery as intolerable.

Among the exhibits is a bus from Montgomery, Alabama. It is possible that this is the very bus in which, in 1955, Rosa Parks refused to give up her seat to a white man, a small event that proved to be a watershed moment, precipitating the American civil rights movement of the 1950s and 1960s. In any event, this is one of the buses the city's black population boycotted in a successful year-long struggle to end segregation, a campaign led by Dr. King. It was the year Montgomery's youngest pastor became world famous.

Preaching in Memphis the last night of his life, King said:

> We've got some difficult days ahead. But it really doesn't matter with me now. Because I've been to the mountaintop. And I don't mind. Like anybody, I would like to live a long life. Longevity has its place. But I'm not concerned about that now. I just want to do God's will. And He's allowed me to go up to the mountain. And I've looked over. And I've seen the promised land. I may not get there with you. But I want you to know tonight, that we, as a people, will get to the promised land! So I'm happy, tonight. I'm not worried about anything. I'm not fearing any man. Mine eyes have seen the glory of the coming of the Lord![30]

From the Lorraine Motel, Therese and I went on to Auction Square, a patch of green with several magnolia trees by the intersection of Auction and Main Streets, just a block or two from the Mississippi River. In the center of the square is its one attraction: a large block of granite, rough on its sides, flat on top. A wrought iron fence now surrounds it. At first glance one wonders what could make this abandoned slab of granite something needing a fence. The answer is as simple as it is shocking: black men, women, and children were exhibited and sold on this small stage during slavery days. Hence the name Auction Street.

The auction stone is a suitable symbol of old Memphis. From its early days this river town was a major location for markets, exchanges, travel, and distribution. Until the defeat of the South in the Civil War, slavery was the economic cornerstone of the region's commerce and agriculture. Nearly all the laborers who farmed the land, raised the buildings, made the roads, and accomplished all the arduous work on the plantations were West Africans, captured and traded as slaves, or their descendants.[31]

Not everyone in Memphis believed slavery was right, but few dared oppose it. It was an issue involving big money and ruthless people.

Our next pilgrimage stop was the Burkle Estate, the household of one local family that had been willing to risk its freedom and well-being to assist runaway slaves trying to make their way to freedom in the North. This one-storey, clapboard house owes it survival to the rundown nature of the surrounding neighborhood.

The house originally belonged to a German immigrant named Jacob Burkle, a successful livestock trader who also opened the first bakery in Memphis. He and his wife must have been people of deep faith with courage to match. Not only did they oppose slavery, but they decided they would help slaves who were seeking freedom. Their house became a stop on the Underground Railroad, a network of clandestine routes used by slaves attempting to escape to free states or go as far north as Canada. Other routes led to Mexico or overseas.[32] The railroad's "conductors" were men and women like Jacob Burkle and his wife.

To better disguise his role, Jacob Burkle owned several slaves. From time to time he would "lose" one or two. Once he was sure they had escaped to safety, he would report them missing.

Several magnolia trees that maintained their green foliage year round provided a useful landmark on the front lawn for escaped slaves trying to identify the Burkle House. The green trees stood out at a distance, no matter what the season.

In recent years the house has been restored and turned into a museum. Each room contains the sort of furniture and decoration that the Burkle family would have owned. Beneath a trapdoor is the cellar, the part of the house where escaped slaves kept out of sight. They slept during the day and left at night on the next leg of their dangerous journey. A narrow, shelf-like structure lines the walls. There are three crawl spaces hidden behind a round wood cover. A tunnel led down to a shack near the shore of the Mississippi River where Mr. Burkle had a boat waiting to take the escapees north.

Some additions in the hallway were surely not part of the original decor. These include a bloodstained whip used to punish disobedient slaves, handcuffs and chains, posters advertising the sale of slaves, and notices offering rewards for escaped slaves. Because of the near match to my family name, the retired school teacher who was our host and guide gave me a photocopy of one of the posters.

FORREST & MAPLES
SLAVE DEALERS
87 Adams Street
Between Second and Third
MEMPHIS, TENNESSEE
Have constantly on hand
the best selected assortment of
FIELD HANDS, HOUSE SERVANTS & MECHANICS
at their Negro Mart, to be found in the city.
They are daily receiving from Virginia,
Kentucky and Missouri, fresh supplies
of likely Young Negroes.
NEGROES SOLD ON COMMISSION,
and the highest market price always paid for
good stock. Their jail is capable of containing
Three Hundred, and for comfort, neatness and
safety, is the best arranged of any in the Union.
Persons wishing to purchase, are invited to
examine their stock before purchasing elsewhere.
They have on hand at present, Fifty likely
young Negroes, comprising Field hands,
Mechanics, House and Body Servants, &c.

"Fresh supplies. . . . Good stock. . . . Likely Young Negroes." It really isn't that long ago that human beings were for sale in America. Indeed, there are places in the world where the slave trade is still going on today.

The Burkle House provides a reminder not only that Christian people bought and sold slaves, made comfortable in their trade by those who presented the Bible as a pro-slavery book, but also that Christian people rescued and freed slaves, understanding the Bible as a challenge to the established order instead of an endorsement of slavery.

A former synagogue in Alkmaar, a hiding place in Amsterdam, a stop on the Underground Railroad in Memphis—just a few of the countless dark places that remind us, on the one hand, of the power of evil, but on the other hand, the human capacity to risk one's freedom and even one's life in behalf of the other, the stranger, the outsider, the endangered neighbor.

Each dark place is an encounter with Christ's cross and, like the cross, confronts us with painful questions: Are we among that small circle of faithful disciples standing near the cross as an act of solidarity? Or are we among the many who have fled from it for fear we too might get into trouble? Or, even worse, are we among those who watch because we enjoy the spectacle of suffering and death?

The letters of Saint Paul include many reflections on the cross. From ancient times to the present, it has bewildered countless people that the all-powerful God should become incarnate in a vulnerable human body and, still more distressing, submit to a torturous public execution, arms and legs immobilized by spikes while slowly perishing on a cross. How can Immortality die?

Death, especially so ugly a death, was a scandal that a missionary to the pagan world had to address. "Many," Paul wrote in his Letter to the Philippians, "live as enemies of the cross of Christ" (3:18). They seek a comfortable life in this world and a painless path to heaven.

Far from providing his Greek listeners with a Christ who was simply a new philosopher whose death was a matter of little consequence, Paul stressed the crucifixion. "We preach Christ crucified," he wrote to the church in Corinth, "a stumbling block to Jews and foolishness to Gentiles" (1 Cor 1:23).

Even within the church there have been schisms that centered on the cross and its implications. Many Gnostics, though drawn to aspects of the gospel, rejected the idea that Christ had died on the cross. Among early heresies was the idea that Christ was actually an imperishable spirit who only appeared to be a human being. Thus death on the cross was an impossibility. Christ could not die. He had no actual body. No resurrection was needed.

One of the reasons we have a creed is that it was necessary for the church in the fourth century to provide those preparing for baptism with a summary of Christ's life that didn't allow any sharp edges to be blurred. Thus the creed includes the proclamation, "He suffered under Pontius Pilate, was crucified, died, and was buried."

Only in the light of his death, cruel and bloody event that it was, does Christ's resurrection—a sign of our own eventual resurrection—have any meaning.

The cross on which Christ died has ever since been intimately connected with whatever trials a person has to endure in life: frailty, illness, destitution, cruelty, calumny, unjust persecution, torture, and execution. Yet once the connection is made with "the holy and life-giving cross," as the Orthodox call it, our trials are seen not as a dead end but as a door.

I saw the connection between the cross and the resurrection most vividly while a pilgrim in Albania. Albania is the country that, among all the atheist states that existed in the twentieth century, took first prize for the thoroughness of its attempt to suppress not only public worship but every trace of spiritual life, even within the privacy of one's home. Every church, synagogue and mosque was closed. To hang an icon on a bedroom wall, to dye an egg red at Easter time, to make the sign of the cross before a meal—even the smallest gesture suggesting rejection of atheism—could be brutally punished. But when Albania's Communist regime at last collapsed in 1991, it was astonishing how quickly and vigorously religious life resumed. Albania was Europe's poorest and most damaged country; everyone had much to worry about. When Archbishop Anastasios arrived to assess what, if anything, was left of Christianity in Albania, people everywhere were exchanging the Paschal greeting, "Christ is risen!" with the response, "He is risen indeed!"

"Everyone was weeping," Archbishop Anastasios recalls, "and I was not an exception. But these were not tears of grief but rather of joy. The longest and darkest of nights had ended. Now the dawn had arrived."[33]

Thin places are hidden in dark places. As Archbishop Anastasios reminded me time and again during the days we spent together, "The resurrection is not *after* the cross but *in* the cross."

Right Where I'm Standing

*All joy, as distinct from mere pleasure, still more amuse-
ment, emphasizes our pilgrim status; always reminds,
beckons, awakens desire. Our best havings are wantings.*
—C. S. LEWIS, LETTER, NOVEMBER 5, 1959

*He did not stop on the porch . . . but went quickly down
the steps. Filled with rapture, his soul yearned for freedom, space, vastness. Over him the heavenly dome, full
of quiet, shining stars, hung boundlessly. From the ze-
nith to the horizon the still-dim Milky Way stretched its
double strand. Night, fresh and quiet, almost unstirring,
enveloped the earth. The white towers and golden domes
of the church gleamed in the sapphire sky. The luxuriant
autumn flowers in the flowerbeds near the house had
fallen asleep until morning. The silence of the earth
seemed to merge with the silence of the heavens, the mystery of the earth touched the mystery of the stars. . . .
Alyosha stood gazing and suddenly, as if he had been
cut down, threw himself to the earth.*
—FYODOR DOSTOEVSKY, *THE BROTHERS KARAMAZOV*

If here and there in the world there are Jerusalem-like centers that never stop drawing crowds of pilgrims, there is another kind of thin place that may be known only to one
person. These are places where unexpected encounters with
God—personal epiphanies—occurred. These are ordinary
places that appear on no pilgrim maps. Even a street corner

can become a thin spot, a place in which the joy of experiencing God's presence can occur.

In his autobiographical writings Thomas Merton records several experiences of God suddenly opening his eyes in life-changing ways. One of the most significant was his "Fourth and Walnut Epiphany," as it is often called. It happened on March 18, 1958, ten years before he died. Merton was in Louisville on an errand, waiting for the light to change at a busy downtown intersection. To avoid being conspicuous, he was wearing an ordinary suit with clerical collar rather than his black and white monastic robes. Suddenly he was overwhelmed with the realization "that I loved all those people, that they were mine and I theirs . . . even though we were total strangers."

Merton writes that he had awakened from "a dream of separateness, of spurious self-isolation in a . . . world of renunciation and supposed holiness." He found that "the whole illusion of a separate holy existence is a dream" and noted that his "sense of liberation from an illusory difference was such a relief and such a joy to me that I almost laughed out loud." For a moment he had been able to see the image of God in unknown people. "There is no way of telling people that they are all walking around shining like the sun." He had discovered that "the gate of heaven is everywhere." He concluded the passage with the observation, "I have no program for this seeing. It is only given. But the gate of heaven is everywhere."[34]

This sudden epiphany while waiting for a red light to turn green proved to be a turning point in Merton's life. It marked the opening of a greater compassion within him. The consequences became obvious in the years that followed, when we see him reaching out to all sorts of people, becoming a voice for peace and a participant in dialogue both with other Christian churches and with non-Christian religions. He had begun his life as a monk who regarded the monastery as a place of escape from a hellish world only in later life to discover the monastery as a place for welcoming and healing the world.

As he later wrote in the introduction to the Japanese translation of his autobiography:

> I have learned . . . to look back into the world with greater compassion, seeing those in it not as alien to myself, not as peculiar and deluded strangers, but as identified with myself. In freeing myself from their delusions and preoccupations I have identified myself, none the less, with their struggles and their blind, desperate hope of happiness. . . . By my monastic life and vows I am saying No to all the concentration camps, the aerial bombardments, the staged political trials, the judicial murders, the racial injustices, the economic tyrannies, and the whole socio-economic apparatus which seems geared for nothing but global destruction in spite of all its fair words in favor of peace. I make monastic silence a protest against the lies of politicians, propagandists and agitators, and when I speak it is to deny that my faith and my Church can ever seriously be aligned with these forces of injustice and destruction.[35]

Today there is a large brass plaque at the Louisville intersection where Merton had his epiphany. What was a very private thin place in his life has become, since his death, a place of pilgrimage for others.

Personal epiphanies are far from rare. I became more aware of how often they occur when I was teaching at a Catholic girls' college in New Rochelle, not far from New York City.

One day I wrote on the blackboard a sentence from the French novelist and poet Leon Bloy: "Joy is the most infallible sign of the presence of God."

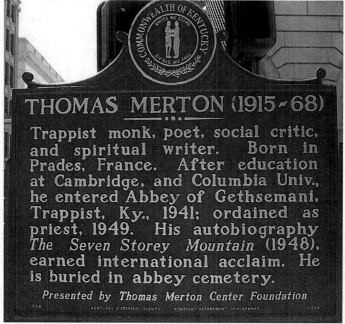

*Plaque at the intersection of Fourth and Walnut
in Louisville*

"Your homework," I said, "is to find time before the next class to write a paper describing a moment of joy in your life–any experience. It isn't necessary that it have an overtly religious context or obvious religious meaning. God often meets us in the most unlikely places, at unexpected moments, and without a neon sign flashing the word *God*."

I suggested adding a second section to the paper exploring the possibility that God was somehow present in that experience of joy. "What did God reveal to you at that moment," I asked, "about who God is, and who you are?"

What is the difference, I was asked, between happiness and joy? I proposed that joy is an experience of wholeness given to us by God, while happiness–a word related to *hap-*

pen and *happenstance*–might be regarded as something more ephemeral, a matter of blind luck, like winning the lottery. Joy is not merely a state of mind achieved by chance or chemistry or good weather; it is a divinely inspired ecstasy that, if only briefly, makes us intensely aware of being loved by God. It is an experience that frees us from fear and all the sins that fear gives rise to: greed, enmity, the inability to forgive. Joy is being blessed by God. It is something that could happen in circumstances that, to a stranger looking on, would seem to rule out joy. You might rarely if ever be happy in a prison, concentration camp, or hospital bed, but you might experience God's joy.

The papers my students handed in the following week were impressive.

One student related an event that had occurred while skiing during a winter holiday when the chronic fear she had been struggling with was abruptly converted to overwhelming delight. She looked back on that experience as "God's reminder to me never to allow fear to have the upper hand in my life." Overcoming another fear, she felt ready to take part in a volunteer project assisting homeless people.

Several wrote about experiencing moments of joy while reading. One student described the impact of reading the autobiography of Dorothy Day, *The Long Loneliness.* "It seemed to me that the desk I was sitting at as I read the book had become a holy place. It suddenly occurred to me that not only did Dorothy Day get through her life without a lock on her door, but that her openness to people that most of us try to avoid made her one of the sanest people in the world. It isn't yet clear to me what exactly I should do with the rest of my life, but I see hospitality as an essential element."

Another student found herself shedding joyful tears as she read a section of Thomas Merton's autobiography, *The Seven Storey Mountain:*

I grew up in a religious family, but by the time I reached my teens I started thinking all the God stories in the Bible were just wishful thinking, something like Santa Claus, and the church a dream factory whose members either pretend to believe or are so stupid they're actually taken in. Merton's book helped me reopen a door I thought I had nailed closed. It makes me laugh to think how attached I had become to those nails! It also changed the way I think about my parents and other people who regularly go to church. We still argue, but I have a lot more respect for them. I can't say I consistently believe in a God who is interested in my life, but there are moments when it's obvious to me that somehow God is present and involved in what's happening.

Several students wrote about the impact of films. One recalled how "The Nun's Story," a film that looked at convent life in a surprisingly straightforward way, had given her a radically new sense of who she was and the direction she should take in life. Leaving the theater, she had been unable just to go home but had walked for at least an hour, "praying without praying while feeling an overwhelming happiness." I asked what that meant. "Prayer without words," she said, "prayer that seemed to come on its own from someplace very deep inside me. I was totally stunned with a sense of God's incredible love. For me, that theater had been, at least for a little while, holy ground."

One student told a story about the relief she had experienced in an act of forgiveness by an estranged friend. "I felt like I had been let out of prison," she wrote. "I had done something I was hugely ashamed of. I couldn't forgive myself. Yet the person I wronged forgave me. It wasn't just a cold word of 'official' forgiveness, but it came right from the heart and brought our friendship back to life. I didn't think forgiveness like that was possible."

Some years later, while teaching at an institute near Jerusalem, I encountered one of my former students, a woman who had subsequently become a nun. She told me the discussion about joy had been an important event in her life. It was, she said, one of the key events "in the pilgrimage that brought me here."

Any place where God meets you becomes at that moment a thin place, while whatever brought you to that spot turns out to have been not just a journey but a pilgrimage. In the case of local pilgrimages that occur along ordinary paths that you follow every day, you don't have to take leave from your job or wave goodbye to your family. No passport is needed.

Such a local epiphany occurred in my wife's life when she was coming home from high school one afternoon. Here is how she remembers what happened:

I was the last lone student on the school bus. I stepped off the bus at my stop, a street corner in an altogether ordinary suburban New Jersey setting, and as the bus pulled away I felt something strange. It was as though I could feel the world as a globe, and I could feel it turning around. I sensed that I was a figure on that globe. I stood still and felt the steady movement of the world, around and around. It was as though I were at the uppermost point, a sort of pole, and the world was turning around on the axis on which I stood. It was such a real feeling that I had to steady myself to keep from falling over. Then I slowly turned around on my axis and gazed at what was visible from where I stood: the four houses on the four corners of the crossroad, the tall pine trees in all the front yards, the mailboxes.

And I realized that there was nobody in the whole world who could see what I was seeing from my great height: not even famous people, not even the President, not even terribly rich people. It wasn't that my view was so special, but I suddenly knew that it was entirely unique.

I went home and told my mother, "Mom, I just felt like I was my own North Pole!" I could understand the vision no further than that at the time. But it remained a fountain of understanding for me. The older I grew the more it revealed to me about myself, about other people, about God. I can say that this vision is the most important thing that happened to me in my life, and I am certain that it was a gift from God who could see that I needed something very big very fast.

Later on in life I began reading about other people who have had similar experiences. It's been like finding out that other people have dreams about missing final exams, when you thought you were the only one.

The experience has haunted Nancy ever since:

My pondering over the polar vision kept me thinking. . . . If I stand on some kind of pole, with longitudinal lines emanating from me and encircling the globe, then those lines must start at some very central point within me. That which is not-me is everything outside that minute central point: my body, my clothing, my surroundings. I must have discovered the existence of my own soul. I must have realized that even when I die, when the not-me is lifeless and gone, that brilliant, living center of light will keep on living.

But what was it? Was it just some little essential version of me? I remembered turning around and around, seeing the suburban homes and the pine trees. Was everything in my life simply there by accident, for me to pick and choose from, or to swallow as gracefully as I could? Was every idea that I grabbed for to explain all this random stuff just that—a convenient idea? Was God no more than a convenient idea? And Jesus? And the whole body of Christian dogma? Could I just shrug if it bored me and turn back to my pure, solitary self?

Finally I knew that what had happened to me on that bus stop was a vision. It was God's way of showing me what it felt like to be free, to be loved and touched by grace. I knew that this experience was something I could hold up to every experience of worship I could have, that it would help guide me to a way of worshiping that was true.

I realized that most people, most of the time, don't choose to stand at that center point. Although it's hard to avoid being where you are physically, most people most of the time want to be elsewhere. Most people imagine that life would be better and they would be happier if only they were out there somewhere, not at the top of the world, not on this lonely North Pole. If only they were wealthier, healthier, better looking, married to someone else, someone else's child, living somewhere else, better educated, more confident, more graceful, more self-assertive; if only it were yesterday, or tomorrow, or in a few years when the children are grown; if only there were a different government, or a different president, or a different social system. Then life would be wonderful; it would be paradise; it would be "heaven."

A very private thin spot sometimes becomes linked with a thin spot that is part of every pilgrim map. In Nancy's case there is a link between that intersection in suburban New Jersey and Mount Tabor in Israel. As she writes:

Toward the end of our time in Israel and Palestine in 1985, we rented a car and drove around Galilee, visiting the holy places around Lake Tiberius, as the Sea of Galilee is called in modern Israel. One of our stops was the towering hill traditionally identified as Mount Tabor mentioned in the Gospel: the site of the Transfiguration.

In a rented car, we drove up the steep, narrow road to the church at the top of the mountain, parked, and went inside. One interesting aspect of this particular church caught my attention: a round circle laid in the stonework floor in the center of the church, with an X transecting it. I went up to this circle and stood in the center of the X, and suddenly it happened again: the polar vision, the unmistakable brush with pure reality. Only this time I found myself standing not on my New Jersey bus stop but on the Pole of Poles: the place where the Lord himself had been transfigured before his disciples.

Of course, the X had been laid in the floor to indicate the place of the Transfiguration. But when I stood there myself and the whole earth fell away from me on all sides, I was able to draw some unavoidable conclusions. . . . The very center of the human individual is God, but we are so confused and distracted by sin that we are almost never able to be there, where we should be, where we are truly ourselves, where God is. If that were possible, we would be transfigured, too. We would shine like the sun.[36]

Leaving Fear Behind

If you are distressed by anything external, the pain is not due to the thing itself, but to your estimate of it; and this you have the power to revoke at any moment.
— Marcus Aurelius

Taking a new step, uttering a new word, is what people fear most.
— Fyodor Dostoevsky

Fear grows in darkness; if you think there's a bogeyman around, turn on the light.
— Dorothy Thompson

I have learned over the years that when one's mind is made up, this diminishes fear; knowing what must be done does away with fear.
— Rosa Parks

I'd never lived more intensely than during those war years. You were constantly filled with fear, but because of that anxiety you could become deliriously happy about the most ludicrous things. After the war, I often missed this intensity.
— A Dutch prisoner held in a
Japanese concentration camp
during World War II

*I*n the mid-seventies my job was editing a monthly journal for a peace organization, the Fellowship of Reconciliation, that has its offices in a mansion in Nyack, a town on the west bank of the Hudson River not far from New York City. The building, Shadowcliff, had been built early in the 20th century by two sisters who had a great deal of money and a terrible fear of fire. Thus the walls, floors, and ceilings were made of reinforced concrete so thick and solid that plumbers and electricians broke many a drill whenever alterations were needed. It is a handsome building—several storeys tall, an outer skin of red brick, a high porch with fluted white columns by the main entrance, and exotic trees on every side of the structure. Inside the massive front door the visitor discovers a lobby resembling the interior of Tara, the mansion in *Gone with the Wind*. Shadowcliff too has a sweeping staircase, an ideal setting for a bride to display her gown and toss her bouquet to a bride-to-be. There is even an organ built into the entrance hall with its pipes tucked away in a curtained crevice in the stairwell.

The setting radiates comfort, wealth, and security, and is thus somewhat at odds with the organization that took possession of the building in the 1950s. Chauffeur-driven cars no longer pass under the columned entrance way. No brides have thrown bouquets from the staircase in decades. Socialites no longer grace Shadowcliff. The organ still works, but it is rarely played. The staff occupying the premises is made up of people who are normally preoccupied with war and social injustice, men and women painfully aware of the world's many ills.

Inevitably such an organization attracts threats. Not everyone regards opposition to war and efforts to overcome enmity as patriotic. Occasionally an angry critic sends an anonymous letter promising violence to those working inside

Shadowcliff. For some reason, 1976 was an especially busy year for such threats. Several letters had been turned over to the police. Many people on the staff were anxious.

It is in the context of repeated threats that one must understand what happened on a warm summer morning in 1976. The receptionist had arrived just before nine to discover a small box by the front door. There was no return address on the brown wrapping paper. While she could hear no ticking inside, it seemed to her a real possibility that the package contained a bomb. She called the police.

Half an hour later several police arrived, carried the box to the lawn behind Shadowcliff, and there opened fire on the box with their revolvers. (Best way to deal with a suspected bomb? Probably not.) There were several direct hits but no detonation. Confident that the box contained no explosives, one of the policemen opened the tattered package.

What did they find? The remains of a note thanking the Fellowship of Reconciliation for its activities for peace and offering a small gift: a rubber stamp with a prayer for peace that has often been attributed to Saint Francis of Assisi:

> *Lord, make me an instrument of your peace;*
> *where there is hatred, let me sow love;*
> *when there is injury, pardon;*
> *where there is doubt, faith;*
> *where there is despair, hope;*
> *where there is darkness, light;*
> *and where there is sadness, joy.*
> *Grant that I may not so much seek*
> *to be consoled as to console;*
> *to be understood, as to understand,*
> *to be loved as to love;*
> *for it is in giving that we receive,*
> *it is in pardoning that we are pardoned,*
> *and it is in dying that we are born to eternal life.*

The stamp, damaged by bullets, was now useless. It was a bizarre fate for a prayer by a saint who had urged Christians to get rid of all their weapons, a saint who had tamed the wolf of Gubbio and crossed the battle lines of the Crusades unarmed in order to meet with an arch-enemy. Francis was a man who was so free of fear and so happy in poverty that he was a scandal to many of his contemporaries.

There are pilgrimages not to geographical places but to healing. More important than a walk to Jerusalem or Santiago de Compostela is the journey from fear to . . . what? That depends. It could be a journey toward greater love, deeper faith, more intimate communion, a pilgrimage toward community, a search for a greater degree of peace within oneself, or simply a quest for the kingdom of God. It is easier to identify the fears we would like to leave behind than name what will take their place. What is clear is that no one aspires to be trapped in a fear-centered life.

We live in an age of pandemic fear. In many lives fear has become an alarm clock ringing continuously each and every day. A few seconds per day are more than enough for an alarm clock to serve its function. Full-time ringing shatters the nerves.

Think of all the things that put us in a state of anxiety. Fear of violence. Fear of bombs. Fear of pathological killers. Fear of terrorists. Fear of war. Fear of toxins in the air and water. Fear of environmental collapse. Fear of job loss. Fear of poverty. Fear of illness. Fear of death. Fear of strangers, lunatics, fanatics. Fear of neighbors.

Only a few years ago many elderly people died in a summer heat wave in Chicago simply because they didn't dare leave their apartments. They were so afraid of muggers that they couldn't get to the air-conditioned shelters the city had provided. They died of fear.

Dig into any social ill, and at the bottom of the hole you will find fear.

In his essay "The Root of War Is Fear" Thomas Merton explored a simple insight:

> At the root of all war is fear, not so much the fear people have of one another as the fear they have of everything. It is not merely that they do not trust one another: they do not even trust themselves. If they are not sure when someone else may turn around and kill them, they are still less sure when they may turn around and kill themselves. . . . It is not only our hatred of others that is dangerous but also and above all our hatred of ourselves: particularly that hatred of ourselves that is too deep and too powerful to be consciously faced. For it is this which makes us see our own evil in others and unable to see it in ourselves. . . . Only love—which means humility—can exorcize the fear that is at the root of war.[37]

I was on the staff of the New York Catholic Worker community when Merton sent the manuscript of that essay to us—a major event in our lives, as Merton was easily the best known Catholic writer in America, while *The Catholic Worker* was the most controversial Catholic publication.

Merton's essay was published in the October 1961 issue, the cover of which was graced with a drawing of Saint Francis, October 4 being Francis's feast day. I mailed a copy to my father, a Marxist. I wanted him to see that not only people on the Left were concerned about war, but Christians too. Not many days later I received his response. My father (who had been a Catholic in his youth) knew of Merton and was impressed to find him writing for *The Catholic Worker*. He found it encouraging to see a person of such stature addressing questions of war and peace. But he said he could not agree with the main thesis.

"The root of war," he said, "is bad economics."

This was the answer I expected—indeed, I could see that, to a considerable extent, it was a sensible response. It is along the lines of Saint Paul's observation that "the love of money is a root of all kinds of evil" (1 Tm 6:10). But then there is the question: what is it that drives the love of money?

Did I write my father to carry the discussion further? Probably not. Too many other things were happening in my life. I regret to say that in those days letters to my parents were few and far between.

I only discovered that my father still had Merton's essay on his mind a decade later, when I received a letter in which he told me, "You know, I still think about what Father Merton said in the essay you sent me and just want you to know that I have come to realize that the root of bad economics is fear."

This was a huge breakthrough for my father—a big step beyond the borders of ordinary Marxism.

In 1985 Nancy and I spent several months living in an ecumenical center, Tantur, between Jerusalem and Bethlehem. One day, Nancy went to an artist's studio in the Old City and stopped to have her portrait drawn—it was her plan to save it as a gift for my birthday. The artist, Elie Schwartz, was in no hurry about the drawing. Nancy must have sat in front of him for two hours or more. While at work, he asked Nancy various questions to draw her out and see her inner self more clearly.

One of his questions proved to be life changing. He asked her what she feared most. Her first answer was nuclear war. It was a time when nuclear war seemed far from unlikely. She mentioned that she had repeatedly had nightmares about a nuclear holocaust. But the artist said: "No, I don't believe you. That can't be right. That's not your deepest fear. Tell me something more personal." Nancy thought and thought. Finally it dawned on her. "What I fear most is getting to the end of my life and realizing that I have been too fearful—too careful–that I never really used my talents." "That's it," the artist said.

It may sound like a small discovery, but it was part of a process of deep change for both of us that took root during those months. Everything we have done in the years since then owes something to that providential conversation. In the weeks and months that followed we made a series of decisions that were quite risky–decisions many would regard as imprudent. I gave up the full-time job I had in order to live as a freelance writer and editor, while Nancy began to work as a freelance translator. Somehow–amazingly–it has worked. There have been times of worry and occasional sleepless nights, yet we have never regretted the steps we took. For both of us it was a leap through the barriers of fear.

The struggle with fear in our own lives made us more sensitive to the issue of fear in the world we live in.

One indication of rising fear levels in many societies has been the rapid increase in the sale of drugs that help people cope with anxiety, depression, and sleeplessness. In the weeks following 9/11, the sale of such drugs was said to have shot up more than twenty percent in New York and Washington, and on similar levels throughout the country. The fear generated by 9/11 remains pervasive and has been deliberately manipulated for political effect, complete with color-coded threat levels. Many are afraid to travel. Fear of strangers is more widespread. Many people who had once been horrified that there are still countries in the world in which torture is allowed now find themselves accepting torture as a reasonable part of the "war on terrorism" and assume anyone accused of being a terrorist must be guilty. One of the legal rights that had been most important to the founders of the United States, *habeus corpus*, has been scrapped.

"People are feeling a bit more vigilant, a little less safe and a little more vulnerable," Robert J. Ursano, chairman of the psychiatry department at the University School of Medicine in Bethesda, Maryland, told a reporter from *The Washington Post.* "It's as if you had broken your leg and you just had the cast taken off. You're very careful where you walk."[38]

Fear is sometimes appropriate. We find ourselves in the path of a car, and the fear we experience is part of a response to get out of the way. But fear also can be packaged and sold. Fear-promoting propaganda comes from many directions, affirmed by "experts" whom one assumes are sober and truthful people in a position to know.

We saw the role of fear in creating a "preemptive" war in its plainest possible form in the US-led attack on Iraq in 2003, a war many reluctantly came to support as a necessary measure, having been assured by America's leaders that Iraq possessed an arsenal of weapons of mass destruction that Saddam Hussein was poised to use against his enemies. "Facing clear evidence of peril," said President Bush, "we cannot wait for the final proof—the smoking gun—that could come in the form of a mushroom cloud."[39] Voices of reason, like that of the former weapons inspector and Marine officer Scott Ritter, were ridiculed or ignored. After Iraq was bombed, invaded, and occupied, it turned out there were no weapons of mass destruction. They had existed only in our fear-ridden imagination.

Driven by fear, we went to war, killing many thousands of people, gravely wounding many more, and destroying countless homes and work places. As this is written, the bloodshed in Iraq is far from over. The vast majority of victims have been noncombatants.

We fear not only real and potential enemies, but also the weapons we ourselves possess that are meant to intimidate our enemies. Those living in nuclear-armed states have created engines of annihilation that are so terrifying as to numb the imagination. The United States, Russia, France, Britain, China, India, Pakistan, North Korea, and Israel possess nuclear weapons. Since the bombing of Hiroshima and Nagasaki in 1945, there have been many close encounters with nuclear war, some intentional, others due to technical error. It is astonishing that none of the close calls has yet resulted in a catastrophic nuclear event.

There are also biological and chemical weapons with vast potential to kill.

There is also widespread fear of environmental damage so massive that large parts of the inhabited world would either be submerged by rising oceans or be subject to ruinous climatic conditions. Some fears motivate urgent corrective responses, but in this case the fear seems numbing rather than empowering. Changes in social structures and personal lifestyle that would protect the environment seem the exception rather than the rule.

Great fears would confront us no matter what age or culture we belonged to, but it happens we live in the "information age"–a culture of mass communication. No generation in history has known so much about what is going on in the rest of the world. Much of the communication that reaches us daily is about frightening events: armed robberies, rapes, pedophiles setting traps for children on the Internet, random murders, attacks in classrooms, highway accidents, outbreaks of disease, wars in progress, earthquakes or other natural disasters, and on and on. As editors in the newspaper trade say, "If it bleeds, it leads." Is there a front page of any daily newspaper that has nothing to do with bloodshed? Or a television news program? Equally disturbing are the films and TV dramas that struggle to outdo one another in the graphic depiction of every form of mayhem and cruelty. Then there are the countless computer games that center on acts of violence. These all contribute to the creation of a fear-driven society.

The fears we are speaking of are all mega-fears: fears that have emerged in the past century with the gradual development of systems, technologies, and methodologies that literally threaten life in earth. But there are other more traditional fears that all of us face on a more intimate scale: hunger, poverty, failure of primary relationships, crime, illness, plague, unemployment, ridicule.

Our fears motivate us to make choices that we think may make us safer. We may opt for a course of studies not out of particular personal interest in the subject but because we think a degree in a particular field is more likely to get us a well-paid job. We may opt for living in a "more secure" neighborhood or even in a "gated community." We may avoid certain areas and types of people. We may vote for politicians who promise to lock up ever more people, keep them isolated from society for longer and longer periods, and advocate "zero tolerance." We may become fervent advocates of the death penalty, even though there is little evidence to suggest that executions have any impact on the homicide rate. We may embrace dehumanizing caricatures of the poor, claiming that they are lazy and dishonest, milking the system for all it is worth, and so on. We may buy cars that have a combat-ready appearance: Hummers, Jeeps, SUVs.[40]

One of the most vivid signals of rising fear is the number of people buying weapons for self-defense. While weapons can make people feel more secure, in reality they increase the risk of violent death for the owner or members of the owner's family.

One of the nightmares that inspires gun purchases is the possible invasion of one's home by a killer armed with a deadly weapon. Such events, though rare, do occur. But does a deadly weapon make one safer? Not necessarily. In fact it could easily make a dangerous situation even worse.

Here is the story of how one unarmed elderly couple responded when a man with a gun appeared in their home one day in February 1984. It is a story—still unfolding—of the pilgrimage from fear.

At the center of the story is Mrs. Louise Degrafinried, seventy-three years old at the time, and her husband, Nathan. They lived near Mason, Tennessee, a rural community northeast of Memphis. Both were members of the Mount Sinai Primitive Baptist Church. The other key participant is Riley Arzeneaux, a former Marine sergeant who was serving a twenty-five-year prison term for murder. Along with four other inmates, he had escaped from Pillow State Prison several days before. Somehow the group obtained weapons. Once on the run, Riley went his own way. The police were in active pursuit both in cars and helicopters—a massive manhunt. Riley had been sleeping rough. It was winter. There was ice on his boots. He was freezing and hungry.

Having come upon the Degrafinried home, Riley threatened Louise and Nathan with his shotgun. He shouted, "Don't make me kill you!"

Here comes the astonishing part. Louise responded to their uninvited guest as calmly as a grandmother might respond to a raucous grandchild playing with a toy gun. She started out by identifying herself as a disciple of Jesus Christ. "Young man," she said, "I am a Christian lady. I don't believe in no violence. Put down that gun and you sit down. I don't allow no violence here."

Riley put the weapon on the couch. He said, "Lady, I'm hungry. I haven't eaten in three days."

Louise calmly asked Nathan to please get dry socks for their guest while she made breakfast. Within a few minutes she prepared bacon and eggs, toast, milk and coffee, setting the table not only for Riley but for Nathan and herself. A striking detail of the story is that she put out her best napkins.

When the three of them sat down to eat, Louise took Riley's shaking hand in her own and said, "Young man, let's give thanks that you came here and that you are safe." She said a prayer and asked him if there was anything he would like to say to the Lord. Riley couldn't think of anything, so she suggested, "Just say, 'Jesus wept.'"

Later a journalist asked how she happened to choose that text. She explained, "Because I figured that he didn't have no church background, so I wanted to start him off simple; something short, you know."

The story crosses yet another border with a confession of love. After breakfast Louise held Riley's hand a second time. She had asked about his family and learned of the death of his grandmother. Riley, trembling all over, said that no one in this world cared about him. "Young man, I love you and God loves you. God loves all of us, every one of us, especially you. Jesus died for you because he loves you so much."

All the while the police had been searching for the Riley and the other convicts. Louise had been on the phone when Riley arrived. As a result of the abrupt ending of the call, the friend she had been talking with alerted the police. Now they could hear the approaching sirens of police cars.

"They gonna kill me when they get here," Riley said. Louise told Riley to stay where he was while she went out to talk to the police.

Several police cars had surrounded the house. Guns ready, policemen had taken shelter behind their cars in expectation that Riley might open fire on them. Instead, they found themselves face to face with Louise Degrafinried. Standing on her porch, she spoke to the police exactly as she had spoken to Riley. "Y'all put those guns away. I don't allow no violence here."

There are people who have a voice-from-heaven authority. The police were as docile in their response to this determined grandmother as Riley had been. They put their guns back in their holsters. With their arms around Riley, Louise and Nathan escorted their guest to one of the police cars. He was taken back to the prison. No one was harmed.

The story of what happened to two of the other escaped convicts is a familiar tragedy. They came upon a family preparing a barbecue in their backyard. The husband, having heard about the escaped prisoners on the radio, had armed himself with a pistol. He tried to use it but was himself shot dead. The men took his wife hostage, stole the family car, and managed to drive out of the state before they were captured and the widow was freed. Another of the five, Ronald Lewis Freeman, was killed in a shoot-out with police the following month.

The Degrafinried story does not end with Riley's return to prison. Louise and Nathan were asked to press charges against Riley for holding them hostage but refused to do so. "That boy did us no harm," Louise insisted. As both she and Nathan refused to testify, the charges were dropped.

Thanks to the Degrafinrieds, Riley's life was not cut short, though twenty more years were added to his prison sentence for having escaped. Louise initiated correspondence with Riley. She asked for his photo and put it in her family album. Throughout his remaining years in prison—he was freed in 1995—Louise kept in touch with Riley, and he with her. Louise actively worked for Riley's release. "He usually called on her birthday and around Christmas time," Louise's daughter, Ida Marshall, related to a journalist after her mother's death in 1998. It was Ida Marshall who wrote Riley with the news of Louise's death.

Louise had enormous impact on Riley's life. "After looking back over all my life in solitary, I realized I'd been throwing my life away," he said in a 1991 interview. Riley recalls praying with Louise Degrafinried when she came to visit him in prison. "She started off her prayer," he recalled, "by saying 'God, this is your child. You know me, and I know you.'" "That's the kind of relationship I want to have with God," Riley said. In 1988 Riley became a Christian. "I realized," he explained, "that meeting the Degrafinrieds and other things that happened in my life just couldn't be coincidences. After all that, I realized someone was looking over me."

Louise Degrafinried was often asked about the day she was held hostage. "Weren't you terrified." "I wasn't alone," she responded. "My Savior was with me and I was not afraid."

It's similar to a comment Riley made when explaining the events that led to his conversion. "Mrs. Degrafinried was real Christianity," he told mourners at her funeral. "No fear." Riley sat in the front pew at the service and was among those carrying Louise Degrafinried's coffin to its burial place.

Riley Arzeneaux now lives in Nashville, where he works as a foreman of a tent and awning company. He and his wife have a son. Not long ago Riley was invited to tell his story to the children of a local primary school in Mason, Tennessee, whose principal is one of Louise and Nathan's children.

The story hasn't yet reached an ending. The consequences of that extraordinary encounter in Mason back in 1984 are still underway. Thanks to the welcome extended by two elderly people, no guns were fired at the Degrafinried house. No one looks back on that day with regret or grief. A man who might have remained a lifelong danger to others has instead become a respected member of society and a committed Christian. Louise and Nathan have died, but their pilgrimage from fear continues to touch the lives of others.

In traditional Christian art there are several icons that have to do with the pilgrimage that begins with fear and ends in the security of the kingdom of God. One of the most potent is the image of Saint George in combat with a dragon.

Little reliable information about George's life has come down to us. All we know is that he was a convert to Christianity who may have been an officer in the Roman army. What marked him out was a public profession of his Christian faith during the time of the persecution of the emperor Diocletian, who reigned from 284 to 305. It was a period

when it would have been prudent to remain silent and hope for better days. One of many martyrs of the time, his fearless witness led to the conversion of many and gave renewed courage to others who were already baptized.

The historical George never saw a dragon. His battle was with an emperor intent on crushing Christianity, a ruler with fear-inspiring powers who could condemn a man to death by the movement of an irritated eyebrow. To disobey the emperor was not unlike participating in combat with a fire-breathing dragon.

In the first millennium, icons of George show him face on, a young man dressed as a Roman soldier. The icon with the dragon came centuries after George's death.

In the medieval period a knightly legend full of rich detail grew up around the image of George battling a dragon. According to the *Legenda Aurea*, written in the thirteenth century by Blessed James de Voragine,[41] archbishop of Verona, the dragon lived in a lake near the city of Silene in Libya. The terrified local people fed him their children to subdue the dragon's rage, just as parents throughout history have so often sacrificed their children in the fires of war. In the tale the children were chosen by lot. It happened that the king's daughter was to be sacrificed. Accepting her fate stoically, she was going toward the lake to meet her doom when a young knight on a white horse, George, happened to be passing. He "drew out his sword and garnished him with the sign of the cross, and rode hardily against the dragon which came towards him, and smote him with his spear and hurt him sore and threw him to the ground." Afterward he asked the princess to tie her belt around the neck of the wounded creature and lead him into the city. The dragon followed, says the *Legenda Aurea*, "as if it had been a meek beast and debonair." After this the king offered Saint George "as much money as there might be numbered," but he refused, asking instead that it be given to poor people for God's sake. The only reward George sought was that the people of the town would accept baptism. "He enjoined the king four things, that is, that he should endow churches, honor the priests, hear church services diligently, and have pity on the poor people, and after, kissed the king and departed."

The story's main point is not battle but conversion: the dragon subdued, the local people freed from fear and brought to baptism, the king converted to a rule of charity and mercy.

It is only after this chronicle that the more ancient, dragonless story is related by Blessed James de Voragine:

Now it happened that in the time of the emperors Diocletian and Maximian persecution of Christian men was so great that within a month 22,000 were martyred. The dread was so great that some denied and forsook God and sacrificed to idols. When St. George saw this, he left the uniform of a knight, sold all that he had and gave it to the poor, and took the habit of a Christian man, and went into the middle of the city and began to cry: "All the gods of the pagans and gentiles are devils. My God made the heavens and is the true God." For this he was arrested, tortured and executed.

The icon of Saint George slaying the dragon is a simple but powerful image of the struggle to overcome whatever inspires fear, symbolized by the dragon. The horse George rides is a graceful creature, as light as air and as fearless as his rider, a visual metaphor of courage given to us by the Holy Spirit. If you study the icon, note that the pencil-thin lance (often with a cross at the top) is not tightly grasped but rests lightly in George's hand, meaning that it is the power of God, not man and his weapons, that overcomes evil. Notice too that George's face shows not a trace of anger, hatred, or anxiety. He is free from passions. Also notice the divine hand extended from heaven in a sign of blessing;

God is with those who struggle to overcome fear in their combat with evil, a combat that seeks conversion rather than destruction.

Another icon to consider is Christ harrowing hell, one of the Paschal icons, the principal feast on the Christian calendar. On Holy Saturday, and often during the week that follows, it is displayed on the icon stand in the center of any Orthodox church. "You have descended into the abyss of the earth, O Christ," the Orthodox Church sings at Pascha, "and have broken down the eternal doors which imprison those who are bound, and like Jonah after three days in the whale, you have risen from the tomb."

One of the affirmations contained in the Apostles' Creed is that Christ "descended into hell." It is a profoundly mysterious event occurring between his crucifixion and resurrection. The best attempt I know of to give this mystery an image is provided by the icon. My favorite example is a fresco on the ceiling of the Church of the Savior at Chora in Istanbul, which Nancy and I visited on Good Friday a few years ago.

In the icon we see Christ standing on the shattered doors of hell, a kingdom of the dead that had been ruled by the prince of darkness, Satan. The figures to the left and right of Christ being raised from their tombs are Adam and Eve, the parents of the human race, while behind them are gathered kings, prophets and other righteous ancestors: David and Solomon, Moses, Daniel, Zechariah, and John the Baptist. The scene implies that all who have died were inmates of this sealed empire. Beneath the gates of hell we see Satan, warden of hell, plummeting into an abyss of darkness amid broken locks and useless keys.

The icon provides an image for the most radical reversal one can imagine—the undoing of the kingdom of death, and thus the undoing of all that keeps us in a state of fear. After all, it is death we fear and spend our lives resisting and delaying. It is fear of death that stands in the way of actually living. Dig away at other fears, and sooner or later we discover the grave. Day by day we come closer to death, traveling at a speed we can only guess. Sooner or later we die. Period. End of story. Whatever delays we manage to arrange, unless we should be witnesses to the Second Coming, the event is certain. Death has the last word, while the final power of those in charge is the power to kill. Displease the powerful, and you may pay with your life.

But, in fact, Christ's resurrection, and in its wake our own, is the ultimate surprise ending. The gates that seemed capable of imprisoning the dead throughout eternity are, it turns out, reduced to ruins. Christ—in a radiant robe and surrounded by a *mandorla*, a symbol of glory and shining truth—arrives among the dead as both conqueror and rescuer. In some versions of the icon there is a scroll in his left hand. When the inscription is shown, it reads, "The record of Adam is torn up, the power of darkness is shattered."

Think of the blame that Adam and Eve, our mysterious original ancestors, have been made to bear in many interpretations of the Bible. All would be well in the world had it not been for their choices in the Garden of Eden. Behind every child dead of starvation, behind every corpse left on the battlefields, behind every murder and rape, there is that original sin committed by our first parents, a primary earthquake in the moral order that is still reverberating in every human life.

Surely they are the very last people to receive Christ's mercy. If anyone belongs in hell, surely it must be Adam and Eve. And yet they are the first people Christ rescues.

Adam and Eve—so much like us! We too are constantly drawn to forbidden fruit hanging from the tree of knowledge. We too make dreadful choices. We too are eager to blame others while exonerating ourselves. In fact, we live in a culture in which blame has become an industry keeping thousands of lawyers occupied full time, while accusing fingers point toward parents, spouses, teachers, neighbors, pastors, bosses, doctors, Hollywood, the mass media, big business, the government. It is nothing new. Adam blamed Eve, and Eve blamed the snake.

Yet Adam and Eve are raised by the Creator's hands from the tomb. It is an action of breathtaking love and mercy. The icon doesn't explain Christ's mercy or justify it.

If the radical failure of Adam and Eve in paradise represents the primary catastrophe in human history, from which all alienation, division, and cruelty has its source, surely this image of divine mercy toward them must be a source of consolation to everyone living in hope of God's mercy. "Delivered from her chains," comments an ancient Paschal hymn, "Eve cries out in her joy." And so may we.

It is only after his conquest of hell that Christ returns to his despairing disciples. "When he had freed those who were bound from the beginning of time," wrote Saint John of Damascus, "Christ returned from among the dead, having opened for us the way of resurrection."

The icon of Christ's descent into hell can be linked with an ongoing pilgrimage to move away from a fear-centered life. We live in what is often a terrifying world. Being fearful is a reasonable state to be in. A great deal of what we see and hear seems to have no other function than to push us deeper into a state of dread.

We can easily get ourselves into a paralyzing state of fear that is truly hellish. The icon reminds us that Christ can enter not just some other hell but the hell we happen to be in, grab us by the hands, and lift us out of our tombs.

It is the pilgrimage of all pilgrimages: being rescued from the kingdom of fear and death by the hands of the risen Christ.

Interruptions and Surprises

We need the interruption of the night
To ease attention off when overtight,
To break our logic in too long a flight,
And ask us if our premises are right.
−ROBERT FROST, "THE LITERATE FARMER AND THE PLANET
VENUS"

An adventure is only an inconvenience rightly considered.
−G. K. CHESTERTON

Some kind of loss is usually necessary to turn the mind toward faith. If you're satisfied with what you've got, you're hardly going to look for anything better.
−FLANNERY O'CONNOR

If we want to be spiritual, then, let us first of all live our lives. Let us not fear the responsibilities and the inevitable distractions of the work appointed for us by the will of God. Let us embrace reality and thus find ourselves immersed in the life-giving will and wisdom of God which surrounds us everywhere.
−THOMAS MERTON, *THOUGHTS IN SOLITUDE*

Pilgrimage, in the sense of a religious journey along an unfamiliar path undertaken on foot, is by definition an extended interruption. Ordinary life, with all its routine actions and well-established schedules, is abandoned. One is no longer due at the office at nine o'clock or expected at home by six. Saturday is no longer a day for shopping and house-cleaning. There are no favorite shows to watch—the pilgrim has no television. The familiar evaporates. Instead of eating meals with family, friends, neighbors, or co-workers, one eats with an acquaintance or two, or with strangers, or alone. Each night one sleeps in a different place. All life's usual tasks, along with one's possessions, have been left in the care of others. A pilgrim's backpack isn't spacious. Indeed, some of the things one was sure were absolutely necessary end up being given away or thrown away after having to carry them for several days. The sweat required is more than they're worth. For pilgrims on the classic transnational routes, even one's customary language is among the things that get left behind sooner or later. In a Spanish, Israeli, or Palestinian village, communication will often be more a matter of good will, expressed by gestures and body language, than the spoken word. During pilgrimage, interruption becomes a way of life.

Interruption is a word with a negative sound. No one longs for interruptions. You were engaged in doing something—talking with a friend, reading a book, running an errand, quietly thinking, even praying—but were interrupted. Probably you experienced a flash of irritation as a consequence.

Surprise, on the other hand, is a word full of promise. "What a surprise!" you say when something unanticipated but welcome occurs: someone you are glad to see shows up unexpectedly, a nicely wrapped package awaits you when you had no idea it was your anniversary, an item of unforeseen good news comes your way.

Considered with an eye open to providence, many an unwelcome interruption might evolve into a heaven-sent surprise. Whether one looks at the unplanned with an open mind or with brittle resentment reveals a good deal about one's spiritual condition at that moment. Step by step, the pilgrim is attempting to leave irritation behind and to receive interruptions with a sensitivity to God's providence. It is a conversion of perception that resembles Christ's first miracle, turning water into wine at the marriage feast at Cana.

For anyone on pilgrimage, each day contains moments that can be regarded with either grateful acceptance or disagreeable resistance: a sudden rainstorm, the needs of a beggar, a chance encounter with a stranger, a blister that needs tending, an unplanned detour, a locked door, getting lost, losing a necessary item, coping with an irritating companion, and so on. It is all part of being on pilgrimage. Pilgrimage is a school in which we attempt to see God's hand not only in what we hoped for but in what we didn't want to happen. It's the losing method of finding. You start by stripping your needs down to what you think you can carry, and then—by exhaustion, theft, or accident—lighten the load still further. The only plan you have is what path to follow, and even that doesn't work out as you imagined it would.

Far from avoiding the unplanned, the pilgrim has chosen a temporary way of life that provides a continuous parade of unexpected moments and events—a life in which interruptions, or surprises, are the main events. But which is it: interruption or surprise? You decide.

When someone looks back on a pilgrim journey, more often than not the unplanned events along the way prove to have the greatest significance. Actual arrival at the goal of the pilgrimage—walking into the Church of the Resurrection in Jerusalem or the Cathedral of Saint James in Santiago de Compostela—may prove to be an anticlimax. Truly there were many God-kissed moments, but far more often than not they occurred at the most unlikely places or times. Or, if by chance, a great moment occurred at the place you were aiming for, chances are whatever happened occurred in an unexpected way—another transfigured interruption.

The great interruption of all time is the annunciation. A young, unmarried woman in Galilee named Mary was in the midst of what must have been an ordinary day in her life, probably helping her mother, Anne, with a variety of chores, when the Archangel Gabriel appeared to her to ask a question: Would you be willing to bear a son named Jesus? This child will be called the Son of God and will be given David's throne, only in this case his kingdom will have no end.

Mary was not obliged to say yes, but in fact she did.

The archangel's massive interruption of Mary's day became the foundation of an interrupted life—of a life hugely different from what she could have imagined in her wildest dreams. Having said yes, an incomprehensible miracle occurred: the God who had made the stars and planets and formed Adam and Eve became a living presence in her womb, an unborn child with no other father than the Creator, a child who would in time become the Messiah, a child who would one day die on a Roman cross, a child who would destroy the gates of hell, a child who would rise from the dead, a child who would be called Savior.

In icons of the annunciation Gabriel is shown on the left, occasionally standing still and steady as a birch tree, but more often with legs bent and apart, as if bounding toward Mary in a posture suggesting sudden movement. The word *angel* comes from the Greek word for "messenger." As far as human beings have been able to tell, angelic messengers move at the speed of light, or—who knows?—even faster. Their response to God's will is immediate. Thus the artistic convention of showing them with wings, though even that symbol falls short of representing instantaneous motion.

Mary is shown on the right, hands raised in astonishment. Her body language suggests it is the moment when she says, "How can this be, since I have no husband?" Or it is what she says after hearing Gabriel's invitation: "Be it done to me according to your word."

To be allowed to see an angel, a being normally invisible, is fearsome. It's not surprising that, time and again, an angel's first words are "Don't be afraid." Perhaps this means not only letting go of the immediate distress of being face to face with a mysterious and magnificent being who lives continuously in the presence of God, but also not to be afraid of the utterly different life that one will be entering as a result of such an encounter.

We all have interruption stories. Here's one from our family. Twelve years ago Nancy realized she was pregnant. Having another child wasn't something we had in mind. Nancy was in her mid-forties, and I was in my early fifties. Our youngest child, Anne, was on the verge of becoming a teenager. Our vision of the future was abruptly shattered. We realized we would be busy with parenthood at what is normally considered the age of retirement. It was a difficult struggle to welcome this unexpected visitor.

A first step was buying a book of photos that followed the development of a child from conception through birth. It made it easier to see that what at first we experienced as an unwelcome interruption was in reality a miracle: a new life entering the world, another child bearing the image of God, another member of the family. As the Orthodox theologian Fr. Alexander Schmemann has written:

> Every birth, every entrance of a new human being into the world, every life, is a miracle of miracles, a miracle that explodes all routine, for it marks the start of something unending, the start of a unique, unrepeatable human life, the beginning of a new person. And with each birth, the world is itself in some sense created anew and given as a gift to this new human being to be his life, his path, his creation.[42]

Helpful words, yet it still was hard work letting go of an illusory future, one that didn't include another round of parenthood.

Our children helped us move from resistance to acceptance—from interruption to surprise. We had imagined they might be embarrassed to see their middle-aged mother pregnant. Not at all. In fact, they were thrilled at the prospect of a baby in the house. Cait and Anne, eager to have a younger brother, even decided on a name: "If it's a boy, let's name him Oscar." We didn't know the child's sex, but from that moment we had an unborn child named Oscar.

One of the friends who happened to visit at the time was a physician. She asked if Nancy had arranged tests to make sure that the child she was carrying wasn't handicapped. "After all," she said, "you have to be aware that, at your age, there's a significant chance of birth defects, autism, or Down's Syndrome." "But what would we do," Nancy asked, "if we discovered there was a defect?" "Then you could have an abortion," our friend replied. "No," Nancy said, "there will be no abortion, and therefore there's no need for any tests."

It may have been that evening that Oscar became as welcome to his parents as he was to the children we had already.

But Oscar's life was brief. Three months into her pregnancy, Nancy had a miscarriage. Oscar's extremely tiny body was buried in our garden. Many tears were shed. Even so, Oscar's life touched us all profoundly. He helped us cross a border. Oscar was an interruption that became a blessing. He helped us let go of entrapment in ideas about the future that were less substantial than smoke and had nothing to do with God's will.

Oscar also played a role in the life of our doctor friend. Afterward she told us that our decision to unconditionally welcome an unexpected and possibly handicapped child was a turning point in the evolution of her own conscience. She would never again suggest an abortion to others or consider one for herself.

Another story of discovering God's presence in difficult moments concerns our friend Therese Cullen. At the time, she was a university graduate student, though even then she was haunted with the idea of starting a house of hospitality.

Therese went on a pilgrimage to Dorothy Day's grave at Resurrection Cemetery on Staten Island, hoping to find both her calling in life and also inspiration for the thesis she was writing on Dorothy Day and Thomas Merton. When at last she found the cemetery, the sun was setting. The gates had been closed and locked. Not one to give up without a struggle, Therese managed to scale the fence. It took some searching and a call on her mobile phone to Mary House, a Catholic Worker house of hospitality in Manhattan, but at last she was standing before Dorothy's modest gravestone, which bears the simple message "Deo gratias" (Thank God).

Therese did what pilgrims always do when they get where they are going. She prayed, asking for Dorothy's help and courage, with a petition thrown in that she not be arrested for invading the cemetery after hours. Daughter of Ireland that Therese is, she followed the Irish custom of leaving something at the grave–in this case a "Women for Peace" button.

Her prayer completed and evening coming on, Therese again climbed over the fence. On the way down, she fell and fractured her leg. It was a nasty break that has since required at least one round of surgery. She now walks without a cane, but Therese is likely to feel an occasional ache in one knee for the rest of her life.

That day of pilgrimage is now a part of who she is physically. Therese has a knee haunted by a saint. Yet her thesis is written and there now exists in downtown Memphis a large house of hospitality dedicated to Dorothy Day where families in need find a helping hand and a warm welcome.[43] Part of the invisible architecture of the house is Therese's knee–

her "Dorothy Day memorial knee," as friends occasionally call it.

Therese's story is not unlike one that Dorothy Day herself liked to tell of one of the saints she most admired, Teresa of Avila. On one of her many journeys, the donkey-drawn cart Teresa was traveling in tipped over and she fell into a muddy river. Sitting on the rocky stream bed, she heard a heavenly voice speaking to her: "This is how I treat my friends." "Yes, my Lord," she replied without batting an eye, "and that's why you have so few of them." Bruised but undeterred, she went on to found yet another convent of Carmelite nuns. The interruption along the way had only strengthened her resolve.

A frequent traveler in sixteenth-century Spain, Teresa knew from hard-gained experience that life in this world is like "a night spent in an uncomfortable inn." Truly it is. Whether at home or twelve time zones away, each day has its cargo of worries, disappointments, and misunderstandings. There are times of sickness, even grave illness. Beloved people die. Catastrophes occur. Great sins are committed. The future seems less promising than the present. Hell often seems more real, and more proximate, than heaven. Anyone going on pilgrimage will find that while troubles along the way may be different from those at home, they are not less numerous or less challenging.

Still there are certain advantages. The very least a pilgrim far from home gets for an interrupted life is entrance into a world in which keeping careful track of time is pointless. Among the many things pilgrims can leave behind is a wristwatch. Those walking a pilgrim path know all they need to know about time from the length of their shadow on the ground. In the first half of the day it gradually shortens until it hardly exists, and in the second half it slowly lengthens until the pilgrim finds shelter for the night. Half past ten in the morning has no significance. Things happen when they happen. Pilgrims live in the freedom of a world without a minute hand.

It was a way of life I began to learn when, just out of the Navy, I joined the Catholic Worker community in New York City. We attempted to live a planned, somewhat predictable life. The many street people we fed each day could anticipate that the door of St. Joseph's House would open at a certain time and that meals would be on the table at the usual hours. Time had a definite geography. We opened the clothing room on the announced days and hours. There was a period each day for begging or buying meat and vegetables at wholesale markets. There was a time each week when some of us would hand out leaflets protesting preparations for nuclear war to people passing near Manhattan's Civil Defense Office on Madison Avenue. For some of us, morning Mass was an essential element of the day. Some of the community also gathered for the Rosary every afternoon, and again for evening Vespers.

But times were always approximate, and much that happened each day had nothing to do with plans and schedules. In fact, each day was a passage through a labyrinth of interruptions. These might include a problematic guest, an unexpected visitor, an inspector from the Fire Department, an argument between staff members, a fight breaking out among the battered men waiting for a meal, a donor delivering boxes of clothing, or any number of other unscheduled events. If you didn't do well in coping with unplanned events, being part of a house of hospitality wasn't a good idea.

It didn't surprise me at the time, but it impresses me now to recall that, though there were religious symbols—a crucifix and several icons—on the wall of our dining room on the ground floor, the busiest part of the house, we had no clock. Perhaps we had one somewhere upstairs, but I have no memory of it.

Traveling in 1967 with Thich Nhat Hanh, the Vietnamese Buddhist monk, I recall a quiet moment while we stood waiting for an elevator at a university in Michigan. Over the elevator doors was a clock. Nhat Hanh looked at it with interest, then commented, "You know, Jim, there was a time when there would have been a crucifix hanging there, not a clock."

It was a startling thought. Truly clocks are among the primary symbols of our post-religious culture.

It is a pity we have stripped so many walls of their crucifixes and put up so many clocks in their place. We are surely more punctual than our ancestors, but we are spiritually poorer. Contemplating a crucifix, many of our forebears had a different idea of how to make use of time. A crucifix may not tell the hour, but it offers crucial advice about what to do with the moment we are living in. It is time for self-giving love, time to pray, time to let go. It is time to forgive, to remember that Christ gave himself—is giving himself—for the life of the world.

A fifty-year-old Dutch pilgrim walking to Santiago de Compostela made this comment about one of the main aspects of pilgrimage:

> Time and distance are no longer relevant things. You just continue, day after day and mile after mile, and that brings you somewhere. Back home time is the essential thing. As a pilgrim, it's great to feel that you have all the time in the world.[44]

In reality we always have all the time in the world, but in ordinary life there is the illusion of being on a clock-driven conveyer belt and being powerless to leap off. Each hour of the day seems to have been claimed and arranged even before we have gotten out of bed in the morning. There is no time to make good use of interruptions or even to notice either the beauty or the sorrow around us.

Why are good Samaritans so few and far between? Perhaps it is because there are so few people who have time to pause for a stranger in need, or indeed for any unscheduled event. Chronic busy-ness is not a new problem, but has there ever been a time in human history when so many people felt that they had no time?

It seems that the merciful Samaritan didn't experience himself as a prisoner in time's straitjacket. He had the invaluable treasure of freedom within time. He had time to notice and to respond to the wounded man lying in a ditch along the side of the road. He had time to bind his wounds and take him to the nearest inn, promising the innkeeper to take responsibility for any costs that exceeded the money he left in advance. The Samaritan had time to participate in the mercy of God. The others who had passed by were too busy.

The Samaritan is a model pilgrim. Those who passed by the wounded man without helping were mere travelers. The Samaritan was open to interruption, the others were not. One of the marks of a true pilgrim is that a pilgrim will not turn a blind eye and walk past a person in need, determined to cling to his or her plan for the day.

Neither will a pilgrim pretend to be deaf. Regarding the virtue of attentive hearing, there's an old Jewish story told by the Dutch philosopher Abel Herzberg about a *rebbe* who walks into a room where his son is deep in prayer. In the corner of the room is a cradle with a baby inside, crying its lungs out. The *rebbe* asks his son, "Can't you hear? The baby's crying!" The son says, "Father, I was lost in God." And the *rebbe* answers, "If you were really lost in God, you'd be able to hear a fly walking up the wall."[45]

Pilgrimage—whether the sort that involves going long distances in unfamiliar lands or simply being aware of ordinary life as a cradle-to-the-grave pilgrimage—is an invitation to become a person capable of seeing interruptions, most of all those involving the urgent needs of others, as heaven-sent opportunities that have the potential of bringing one closer to the kingdom of God. Whether washing dishes in the kitchen or walking to Jerusalem, life is learning to see interruptions as God's plan for the day rather than one's own plan, and thus to live in God's time rather than clock time.

As Dorothy Day put it:

Paper work, cleaning the house, dealing with the innumerable visitors who come all through the day, answering the phone, keeping patience and acting intelligently, which is to find some meaning in all that happens—

these things, too, are the works of peace, and often seem like a very little way.[46]

Dorothy often used the phrase "little way." It was a reference to one of the main strands in the writings of Saint Thérèse of Lisieux.[47] Thérèse's "little way" centered on doing ordinary tasks, suffering petty insults and injuries, accepting interruptions. It was a way of living in time with the awareness of being in the presence of God, seeing every action as a potential channel of God's love. As Thérèse said with her usual modesty, "I am only a very little soul, who can only offer very little things to our Lord." Yet, as she saw it, every moment accepted and lived in a spirit of love provides an occasion for valor and a step along the path to becoming the saint God intends each of us to become.

If Saint Thérèse of Lisieux was one of Dorothy's sources of wisdom, another was the philosopher and psychologist William James. He too was a champion of the importance of small choices. Dorothy knew this passage from James's writings by heart:

> I am done with great things and big things, great institutions and big success, and I am for those tiny molecular forces that work from individual to individual, creeping through the crannies of the world like so many rootlets, or like the capillary oozing of water, yet which, if you give them time, will rend the hardest monuments of man's pride.[48]

Again, it's the little way, the small-step-by-small-step approach to the kingdom of God. It's the little way that transforms resistance to interruptions into receiving whatever happens to us as an opportunity for conversion.

A final story of how those who follow the little way may find that disappointments sometimes contain epiphanies. An

English pilgrim, having arrived in Santiago de Compostela after many days of walking, went to the Hostal de los Reyes Catolicos for the traditional free meal served three times a day to the first ten pilgrims to arrive. Upstairs a four-star hotel is serving (for a pretty penny) some of the city's best food, while in the pilgrim room below the free food is as plain as the room in which it is eaten. Guests mindful of the elegant repast being enjoyed upstairs often find the free meal in front of them a major letdown. As Bettina Selby writes:

> It seemed the loneliest, most derelict moment of the entire journey. I tried the bean stew and it tasted repulsive, the chicken was exactly as it looked, even the apple was flaccid and flavorless. It was strange that in a country in which the food was so good and inexpensive, the first uneatable meal I was offered was the one that should have been a celebration.
>
> It just left the bread and the wine, and it was as I broke the roll in half that I suddenly knew that this was the moment that had brought the completion of the pilgrimage. Like the unnamed disciples on the road to Emmaus, I too had needed to encounter the reality of the Risen Christ. He had been there in every meeting along the way, and perhaps I had known this in a remote corner of my mind. But to realize it fully had required this ordinary, everyday action in which the symbol could suddenly break free and be recognized for what it was. "They recognized him in the breaking of bread."[49]

The Pilgrimage of Illness

A wise man should consider that health is the greatest of human blessings, and learn how by his own thought to derive benefit from his illnesses.

—HIPPOCRATES

I have never been anywhere but sick. In a sense sickness is a place, more instructive than a long trip to Europe, and it's always a place where there's no company, where nobody can follow. Sickness before death is a very appropriate thing and I think those who don't have it miss one of God's mercies.

—FLANNERY O'CONNOR,
THE HABIT OF BEING,
LETTER DATED JUNE 28, 1956

Any trip, even a small journey from one prosaic location to another, has the potential to become a pilgrimage.

In my own case these last few years, the most common of pilgrimages has been going from our house to the local hospital, a five-minute bicycle ride from our front door. I make that small pilgrimage three afternoons a week, normally on Monday, Wednesday, and Friday.

It's a journey that began several years ago when a routine blood test revealed that the creatinine level in my blood was higher than it should be. Our family doctor referred me for further tests to a specialist at the hospital. More tests made it clear that my kidneys were gradually failing, probably due to damage caused by high blood pressure. Sometime in the not-distant future, the doctor said, I would need to make use of an artificial kidney machine in order to stay alive.

Dialysis was something I passionately wanted to avoid. During the thirty months that followed diagnosis, I faithfully took all the medication my doctor prescribed, but I also looked into alternative treatments. Nancy and I researched diet change. I found a local acupuncturist who made no promises but said acupuncture might help. As a result, I spent many hours with needles placed in various areas of my body, from feet to ears. Perhaps changed diet and acupuncture were factors in retarding the progression of the disease, but tests showed that my kidney efficiency continued to decline.

I often prayed for a healing miracle, and many prayed for me. For several years I have been on a list of people for whom our parish prays at each and every liturgy. The fact that there has been no miracle is disappointing, and yet I have felt greatly helped by prayer. I think it was a major factor in my gradually coming to terms with my illness, an inner shift that happened quite slowly. It may well have been the prayer of others that helped me realize I was on a pilgrimage. For the better part of three years, even while writing earlier chapters in this book on pilgrimage, I'm embarrassed to say such a thought never crossed my mind.

In that period of regular hospital visits and frequent blood tests, far from seeing myself on a pilgrim's path leading more and more deeply into the kingdom of God, it seemed to me that I was simply a victim of rotten luck. Each trip to the hospital was a painful reminder of a dark, confining future that was relentlessly coming my way. While I rejoiced each time my doctor told me that dialysis wasn't yet needed, it was joy with a shadow, as he also made me aware that month by month my creatinine level was slowly but steadily rising, a sure sign of kidney decline.

During each visit to the hospital I had a glimpse into the several wards where patients were undergoing dialysis. It seemed to me a nightmare vision. Transparent plastic tubes filled with dark red blood ran from the bandaged arms of men and women into large machines that looked like props from "Star Wars." I hoped against hope that I would not eventually have to join them.

And yet I have. In January 2006, soon after returning from a Christmas visit with my oldest son, his wife, and their two children in America, my doctor looked at the latest blood test results, then called the dialysis unit to make an appointment for me to start dialysis the next day.

What I had desperately hoped to avoid is now normal. I now spend nearly twelve hours a week–fifty hours a month, six hundred a year–at the dialysis clinic. Dialysis is part of the core structure of each week. Blood-filled plastic tubes now link my arm to a dialysis machine. Nurses that I saw caring for others now care for me. People who were unenviable strangers, dialysis patients, now are people I know by name. The "other" now includes me. We're all in the same boat.

I've had to rethink how best to use my available work time. My work time has been radically cut. This has not been easy.

Yet there are significant pluses to report. It finally dawned on me that the hospital I dreaded visiting is actually holy ground. My main pilgrimage these days is the unprayed-for blessing of regularly going to a place where nearly everyone is sick, caring for the sick, or visiting the sick.

I've discovered that far worse things can happen than being chronically ill. Unlike people burdened with the illusions that come with good health, the sick are well aware that they are unable to survive on their own. We are intensely conscious of our dependence on the care of others. It's hard to be seriously ill and not be poor in spirit, the first

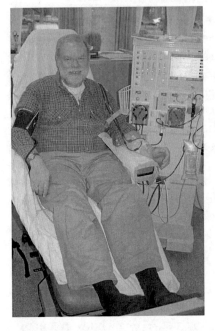

of Christ's Beatitudes. Because of that, the sick are by definition on the ladder of the Beatitudes. Each of us may still have quite a lot of climbing to do, but, thanks to illness, at least we've made a start. We are on the first rung.

In a culture that prizes individuality and independence, most of us are reluctant to realize how much we depend on others, though in reality there has never been a day of our lives when this wasn't the case. We started that dependence the instant we were conceived, and it continues without interruption until we take our last breath. We depend on others for love, for encouragement, for inspiration. We depend on others for food. We depend on others for the words and gestures that make communication possible. We depend on others for all the skills we slowly acquire while growing up. We depend on others for truth and wisdom. And yet for much of our lives we manage to nourish the illusion that we are independent and have the right to pat ourselves on the back for whatever good things come our way. The phrase *thank you,* however often it was said out of social necessity, didn't necessarily reflect a deeply felt attitude.

Being sick changes that. The words *thank you* begin to rise from the depths of the heart. In the community of the sick, there aren't many people unaware of how much they depend on the care of others, even if they don't know most of these others by name. It's not only dependence on the doctors and nurses who directly care for us, but on all those who have such unheralded tasks as doing laboratory analyses in rooms we never enter or quietly keeping the hospital clean or changing the lights.

Directly or indirectly, what all these people are doing day after day is trying to keep us alive a little longer and, in the case of those we meet face to face, even trying to keep our spirits up in the process. They are professional, full-time life savers, yet they do not see themselves as heroes. They do what they do with the matter-of-factness of a teacher writing $2 + 2 = 4$ on a classroom blackboard or a plumber repairing a stopped-up sink. Yes, there are those for whom hospital work seems to be just a job, and perhaps not one they especially like doing; but my experience suggests such people form a small minority.

At the end of a session of dialysis, I sometimes say to the nurse who helped me that day, "Thanks for saving my life." She (or sometimes he) always looks surprised to hear such a declaration. Generally people are too polite to express appreciation that plainly, though anyone with an illness that not long ago was a death sentence knows he or she is living on extra time. Every dialysis patient knows that, without dialysis, he or she wouldn't have long to live. The writer James Mitchner's life ended a week after he decided he had had enough dialysis.

It is not only the professional care-givers who make a hospital holy ground, but also those who visit the sick. Though the regulations in many hospitals restrict visits to predetermined hours that pose the least inconvenience for staff, in practice we find visitors arriving and departing throughout the day and rarely being told to go away. Typically they arrive carrying flowers, though some bring books, magazines, chocolates, juice, balloons, music, or all sorts of other things they hope will communicate their love and give the patient a little extra energy for coping with illness.

It is holy work, often done despite a temptation not to be there. Hospitals, after all, are places exploding with reminders of human mortality. The most death-denying person knows that every day there are people breathing their last in this building. Also, hospitals are not the healthiest places to be in. Yet crowds of people each day manage to overcome their hesitation, even their fear, and cross the border. After all, it's not easy to communicate the bond of love while physically avoiding the person you love. Greeting cards and phone calls aren't bad, but they can never equal the reality of being there.

Visiting is a healing work as crucial and powerful as what the doctors and nurses are doing. There is nothing more healing than love. Love can be expressed far more openly by the visitor than the health-care professional. Whether visitors sit silently or talk nonstop, they manifest how much the sick person they are visiting matters to them. Those who visit the sick are pilgrims, for they are meeting not only someone familiar but Christ as well, who is forever hidden in those who are ill. It was he who said, "I was sick and you visited me."

In my own case, I'm one of the lucky ones within the community of the sick. Kidney illness is certainly inconvenient, and it's not painless being jabbed in the arm with two large hollow needles several times each week. On the other hand, neither the illness itself nor dialysis (once you are connected to the machine) is painful. Kidney illness has become treatable. You can live a long and full life on dialysis. You can even travel, though it is not as easy as one would like setting up appointments for care at places you might wish to visit. You might even be one of the lucky ones who eventually gets a transplant and no longer needs dialysis. (As this is written, Nancy is awaiting the result of the tests to see if she can be a kidney donor.)

But in the meantime, being sick and needing frequent care is not without rewards. If you happen to love books, dialysis gives you the possibility of hours of quiet reading time each week. In my life, that qualifies as an answered prayer. Prefer watching TV? Normally I don't, but there's a TV close at hand should I find myself too tired to read and yet unwilling to take a nap. I happened to catch an excellent program on monastic life the other day. Also, I've been given a small DVD player and occasionally watch a film.

The pilgrimages being made by others who are sick are often much harder than mine, or more difficult to bear. In other sections of the hospital I sometimes encounter children who are gravely ill. I often see people who are in great pain and distress. I see faces collapsing with discouragement and grief. There is usually nothing at all I can do but silently pray, which may in fact be an achievement in the face of the overwhelming powerlessness I sometimes feel when I witness what other people are up against. Prayer seems so meager a response—in moments of doubt, just another form of nothing. But *not* to pray is itself a kind of dying.

Being among the sick is being among those who include the dying. Recently, a frail dialysis patient in his eighties died before my eyes. I thought he had dozed off. So did the nurses. But at the end of his session, when a nurse tried to wake him up, it was discovered that he had quietly left this world. His pilgrimage was ended.

In fact, pilgrimage has always been a dress rehearsal for dying, and for many a direct journey to the grave.

But what better death is there than to die on pilgrimage? Each year pilgrims die of accidents and illnesses. Every pilgrim route acquires memorials to those whose lives were completed along the way. Among the monuments one finds on the way to Santiago de Compostela in Spain is a pilgrim's staff with a rusting bicycle set in a concrete pedestal, its front wheel raised toward heaven. The German who had been riding it died of a heart attack in El Acebo. Later on, an Irish pilgrim happened to find a bouquet of flowers along the roadside, picked it up, but found it awkward to carry. When she came upon the bicycle monument, she left the flowers there. It surprised her to realize that death while on pilgrimage is a blessing. It occurred to her that, like the German biker, she "did not want to spend the last days or months of her life dying in bed."[50]

I recall a priest Nancy and I met at a Russian Orthodox church in Jerusalem who showed us a scrapbook nearly a century old–fading photos of Russian pilgrims coming in the thousands to the Holy Land until such journeys were made impossible, first by the World War that broke out in 1914 and then by the restrictions imposed by the Soviet regime after 1917. He pointed out that many of the pilgrims we saw in the photos had buried others who had died along the way, and that many more died either in Jerusalem or on the way back home.

"A pilgrim leaving Russia in those days never assumed he would return alive the way a tourist does these days," he said. "They said goodbye as if for the last time, as indeed was often the case. But this thought did not disturb them. They saw it as a benediction to die on pilgrimage, and especially to die in the city where Jesus rose from the dead."

Whoever is on the pilgrimage of illness cannot help but be more aware of last things than many others, although the job of the pilgrim is not dying but living. As Saint Irenaeus, one of the theologians of the second century, said, "The glory of God is the human being fully alive."

Even if it is a life of confined borders, it is no less a life.

The Pilgrimage to the Front Door

I was a stranger and you welcomed me.

–JESUS (MT 25:35)

It is cheering to remember that Jesus Christ wandered this earth with no place to lay his head. "The foxes have holes and the birds of the air their nests, but the Son of Man has no place to lay his head." And when we consider our fly-by-night existence, our uncertainty, we remember (with pride in sharing the honor) that the disciples supped by the seashore and wandered through cornfields picking the ears from the stalks wherewith to make their frugal meals.

–DOROTHY DAY,
EDITORIAL IN THE FIRST ISSUE
OF *THE CATHOLIC WORKER*, MAY 1933

The Greeks used to say that people in need are ambassadors of the gods.

–PETER MAURIN,
CO-FOUNDER OF THE
CATHOLIC WORKER MOVEMENT

Blessed are they who have no locks on their door.

–FYODOR DOSTOEVSKY

*O*ver breakfast one morning, Nancy asked me, "What is the most important thing in the house?" I thought first of our icons, then certain treasured books, then works of art that hang on our walls. "That's not it," Nancy said. "The most important thing is the front door. The front door is the place where whoever knocks is made welcome or kept distant. The front door is directly connected to the Last Judgment."

There is no pilgrim who wouldn't agree. Just as important as setting out on a journey is finding open doors and welcoming faces along the way. Without the many hospices along the way, few traditional hotel-avoiding pilgrims following the route to Santiago de Compostela would be able to walk those paths, least of all those with little money. Thousands of people, mainly volunteers, staff the hospices, provide meals, bandage blisters, give advice, tell stories—and listen to them.

But dependence on hospitality doesn't only apply to pilgrims far from home. Each of us depends on the care of others, especially care that is given freely—care that expresses love. Where would I be in life had it not been for the care of others: parents, teachers, friends, co-workers, clergy, and strangers?

The pilgrim, in the sense of a traveler far from home, is by definition an outsider, a stranger. It is no bad thing to be an outsider. The Greek word is *xenos*, which is part of the Greek word for hospitality, *filoxenia*, literally "love of the outsider."

Hospitality is not only a duty but a blessing, and a shared blessing at that. One can speak of the sacrament or mystery (from the Greek word *mysterion*, the Orthodox term for a sacrament) of hospitality. For those with eyes to see, the guest is an angel in disguise, like those heaven-sent angelic guests who were welcomed by Abraham and Sarah under the oak of Mamre.

There are still societies in which one can experience *filoxenia*. In such cultures there is little need for hotels.

In a memoir, Tatiana Goricheva, then a university student living in what was still called Leningrad, recalls going to the village of Pechory, adjacent to one of the few monasteries still surviving in the final years of the Soviet Union. She discovered that all she needed to do to find shelter in this community without hotels was to knock on any door and say, "Lord Jesus Christ, Son of God, have mercy on me, a sinner." The response from the person answering the door was, "Amen!" She immediately became a well-cared-for guest.[51]

Not many years ago, I had a similar experience in a Palestinian village near Haifa in Israel. Though a complete stranger who was simply looking for travel advice, I ended up as an honored guest of a local family who were celebrating a wedding. I sat at the wedding table in the family home and slept that night in the guest room. It is hard to imagine something similar occurring where I grew up (Red Bank, New Jersey) or where I now live (the town of Alkmaar in the province of North Holland). Not that these towns turn a cold shoulder to strangers—not at all—but it is taken for granted that visitors will have made arrangements to stay at a hotel.

I recall a Romanian couple we met after the liturgy one Sunday at our parish in Amsterdam. They had slept the night before in Amsterdam's main railway station and were planning to do the same for a few more nights. Instead, we had the blessing of their staying with us. We became friends and still correspond. One of them was preparing to be ordained a priest; both were working with children who were in foster care. A conference on children with special needs had brought them to the Netherlands, but once it ended they had nowhere to stay before their return journey. What a pleasure it was to have them in our house!

Of course, one has to know one's limits and to practice discernment. One's vocation, other obligations, and the condition of the family are among the factors that have to be taken into account. Hospitality cannot be forced. Yet what a gift it has been for our children, in the years they were growing up, to share our table with so many people from so many countries, from Nobel laureates to backpacking kids, from the sensitive and helpful to the socially clueless and energy consuming.

I recall our daughter Cait one evening being disappointed that we were without a guest and asking: "Isn't there anyone we could invite? Couldn't you call the office?" (At the time I was working for the International Fellowship of Reconciliation.)

When a guest was with us, we would place a world globe on the table so the guest could point out where he or she lived. They came from every continent. Our kids learned geography through hospitality. Just as often we would dig up an old issue of *National Geographic* magazine and ask the guest to tell us about photos taken in his or her homeland.

On one occasion we had a Burmese Buddhist monk staying with us. His burgundy and saffron robes drew several of our neighbors out of their houses one morning simply to stare at our colorful guest.

I recall a guest from Greece named George who turned up at the front door one afternoon. George was in his early thirties. He knew someone in Greece who knew someone who knew us and thus had gotten our address. He had come to Holland because his small business, a camera shop, had failed. He was hoping to find a Dutch job so that he could pay back his debts and support his mother. He ended up staying with us about three months, our longest single experience of hospitality. A good man! Warmhearted, hard-working, resourceful, and always helpful in the house. George was a four-star guest. He too became a friend.

I can't say we look back on every guest with equal gratitude, but I can't think of anyone we would, in retrospect, have turned away, even if we sometimes breathed a sigh of relief on the day of departure.

Doors of welcome open to strangers in every country, though in some societies more often and more joyfully than in others. Sadly, there are many countries in which hospitality is the exception rather than the rule. There are those houses in which welcoming a stranger would be more surprising than pointing a gun at him. Far from appreciating a culture of hospitality, there are those who regard as irresponsible if not insane those who welcome strangers.

One can see practically everything that matters in life in terms of hospitality. Marriage is an act of hospitality: a man and a woman each making space in their life for the other. It is an ongoing crash course in self-giving love versus selfishness. Parenthood too is hospitality. It is hard to think of a more demanding act of hospitality than bearing children and then, once they are born, adjusting one's life to these amazing, unfamiliar guests with their infinity of needs. Perhaps it's in the crucible of family life that we gradually become more capable of welcoming strangers.

The hospitality of marriage is portrayed in the icon of Mary's parents, Anne and Joachim, welcoming one another while behind them are the wide-open doors of two linked buildings.

When asked about my education, occasionally I say I am a graduate of "Dorothy Day University," then correct myself to say I am still attending classes while working on a degree in hospitality. It is a "university" that many attend and from which no one ever graduates. Learning hospitality is a lifetime project.

Despite her death in 1980, Dorothy Day is one of the people who helps us open the front door. It is no wonder so many places of welcome bear her name. She has inspired many to practice hospitality, was herself among the founders of several houses of hospitality, and lived in various houses of hospitality from 1933 until she died. Now she seems to be on her way to being formally recognized as a saint. Her writings continue to influence many people.

Her basic message—borrowed from the gospel—is stunningly simple: we are called by God to love one another as God loves us.

If *God* was life's key word for her, *hospitality* was nearly as important. Again and again she repeated a simple instruction from the early church, "Every home should have a Christ room in it, so that hospitality may be practiced." Hospitality, she explained, is simply practicing God's mercy with those around us. Christ is in the stranger, in those who have nowhere to go and no one to welcome them. "Those who cannot see the face of Christ in the poor are atheists indeed," she often said.

Hardly a day passed in her adult life when she didn't speak about the works of mercy.

The works of mercy—feeding the hungry, giving drink to the thirsty, clothing the naked, giving shelter to the homeless, caring for the sick, visiting prisoners, burying the dead—have to be understood not only in a material but also a spiritual way. There is hunger not only for food but also for faith, not only for a place at the table but also for a real welcome, not only for assistance but also for listening, not only for kind words but also for truth.

There is not only hospitality of the door but hospitality of the face. Dorothy had a face of welcome.

Until old age stopped her, Dorothy traveled a great deal, giving lectures and visiting houses of hospitality. It was a life on pilgrimage, she said. Indeed, her column in *The Catholic Worker* was called "On Pilgrimage," nor did the title change when she was forced to give up travel.

For all her traveling, she was anchored in New York City, where she divided her time between Manhattan and Staten Island. Before her conversion, in 1927, when she was thirty years old, she had bought a small beach house on Staten Island. It was a simple structure with two or three plain rooms and a cast-iron stove. Walking on the beach or to the post office, rosary in hand, she prayed her way through an out-of-wedlock pregnancy, prayed her way through the *Baltimore Catechism,* prayed her way to her daughter's baptism in a nearby Catholic parish, prayed her way through the collapse of a common-law marriage and to her own baptism, prayed her way through the incomprehension of her atheist friends who regarded all religion as snake oil. Years later it was mainly in the beach house that she found the peace and quiet to write her autobiography, *The Long Loneliness.*

The main part of her New York life was in Manhattan with the urban part of the Catholic Worker community. In the early 1960s, St. Joseph's House of Hospitality was on Chrystie Street–a decrepit three-storey building a block from the Bowery, in those days the city's grimmest avenue. As there wasn't enough room inside, the down-and-out were often lined up at the door waiting either for food or clothing–men mainly, people often grouped under the heading "bums." Bums had been a major part of Dorothy's life since leaving college in Illinois to come to New York. Not long before the United States entered World War I, she rented a room on the Lower East Side and, at age eighteen, became a reporter for New York's socialist daily newspaper, *The Call.*

Dorothy's office at the Catholic Worker was hardly big enough for her desk. Here she and I would sometimes discuss–occasionally argue about–what should be in the next issue of the paper. It wasn't the easiest place for conversation.

The ground floor was where food was prepared and meals served, each meal in shifts, as there was room only for a few tables. From morning till night it tended to be noisy. Sitting at her desk one afternoon, talking about the next issue, we could hardly hear each other. Dorothy got up, opened her office door, and yelled "Holy silence!" For a minute or two, it was almost quiet.

On the second floor, site of the two clothing rooms, one for men, one for women, there was an area with several hand-me-down chairs and couches that we used for daily prayer—lauds, vespers, compline—as well as recitation of the Rosary every afternoon. None of this was obligatory, but part of the community was always present, the community being a mixture of staff (as those of us who came as volunteers were called) and family (people who had once come in for clothing, a bowl of soup, or a place to sleep and gradually had become part of the household).

It wasn't a comfortable life. At the time I joined, Dorothy had a sixth-floor walk-up apartment in a tenement on Spring Street. For twenty-five dollars a month she got two small rooms, a bathtub next to the kitchen sink, and a shared toilet the size of a broom closet in the hallway. As uninviting as this may sound, Dorothy regarded living in the Spring Street neighborhood as luxury enough. With an Italian bakery across the street, the smell of bread in the oven was often in the air, and there was always the intoxicating perfume of Italian cooking. The San Gennaro Festival was celebrated annually just around the corner; for a week that part of Manhattan became a village not far from Naples. (You get a glimpse of the district and its San Gennaro Festival in the second of the *Godfather* films.)

The day at last came when climbing those five flights of stairs became too much for her aging knees, so we helped her move to a similar apartment on Ludlow Street, a few blocks away, in which she would have to climb only one flight of stairs—another cold-water flat, but in a seedier neighborhood. The place was in appalling condition. Stuart Sandberg and I went down to clean and paint the two rooms, dragging box after box of old linoleum and other debris down to the street, including what seemed to us an awful painting of the Holy Family—Mary, Joseph, and Jesus rendered in a few bright colors against a battleship-gray background on a piece of plywood. We shook our heads, deposited it in the trash along the curb, and went back to work. Not long after, Dorothy arrived carrying the plywood painting. "Look what I found! The Holy Family! It's a providential sign, a blessing." She put it on the mantle of the apartment's bricked-up fireplace. Dorothy had a gift for finding beauty in unlikely places—the eyes of a pilgrim.

She was one of the freest persons alive, yet also one of the most disciplined. This was most notable in her religious life. The sacraments were the bedrock of her existence. Whether traveling or home, it was a rare day when Dorothy didn't go to Mass, while on Saturday evenings she went to confession. What could she possibly have to confess, I once asked her. "My awful temper," she replied.

She never obliged anyone to follow her example, but God knows she gave an example. When I think of her, the first image that comes to mind is Dorothy on her knees praying before the Blessed Sacrament either in the chapel at the Catholic Worker farm or in one of several urban parish churches near the Catholic Worker. One day, looking into the bible and missal she had left behind when summoned for an urgent phone call, I found long lists of people, living and dead, whom she prayed for daily. There was a special list for those who had committed suicide.

Occasionally she spoke of her "prayings": "We feed the hungry, yes," she told her friend Bob Coles. "We try to shelter the homeless and give them clothes, but there is strong faith at work; we pray. If an outsider who comes to visit us doesn't pay attention to our prayings and what that means, then he'll miss the whole point."[52]

As tends to be the case with pilgrims, she was attentive to fast days. It was in that connection that she told me a story about prayer and fasting. For many years, she said, she had been a heavy smoker. Her day began with lighting up a cigarette. Her main sacrifice every Lent was giving up smoking, but having to get by without a cigarette made her increasingly irritable as the days passed, until the rest of the Catholic Worker was praying she would light up a smoke. One year, as Lent approached, the priest who ordinarily heard her confessions urged her not to give up cigarettes that year but instead to pray daily, "Dear God, help me stop smoking." She used that prayer for several years without it having any impact on her addiction. Then one morning she woke up, reached for a cigarette, and realized she didn't want it. She never smoked again.

People sometimes tell me how lucky I am to have been part of the community while Dorothy was alive and active. They picture a group of more or less saintly people having a wonderful time doing good works. In reality, Catholic Worker community life in Manhattan in the early 1960s had much in common with purgatory. The staff was made up of people with very different backgrounds, interests, temperaments and convictions. We ranged from the gregarious to the quiet. Foremost among the latter was a recluse named Keith living in a back room on the third floor who maintained the mailing list—a big job, because *The Catholic Worker* had nearly a hundred thousand subscribers. He was rarely seen and never in my hearing said a word. Communication with him was by notes.

There was lean, gentle, long-suffering Charlie Butterworth, a lawyer who had graduated from Harvard but whose objection to war had led him to the Catholic Worker. Arthur J. Lacey, with his matchstick body, was chiefly responsible for the men's clothing room; he called himself "Haberdasher to the Bowery." There was Stanley Vishnewski, our resident comedian, who said we belonged "not to the Catholic Worker movement but to the Catholic Shirker movement." No one in the community apart from Dorothy had been there so many years as Stanley.

Agreement within the staff was as rare as visits by the president of the United States. The most bitter dispute I experienced had to do with how best to use the small amounts of eggs, butter, and other treats that sometimes were given to us—serve them to "the line" (people we didn't necessarily know by name who lined up for meals) or the "family," as had been the custom. Though we worked side by side, saw each other daily, and prayed together, staff tension had become too acute for staff meetings. When Dorothy returned from a speaking trip she told the two people then running the kitchen that the butter and eggs should go to the family, as before. This led to their resigning from kitchen work and soon after leaving the community, trailing black smoke, convinced that the actual Dorothy Day wasn't living up to the writings of Dorothy Day.

One of the miracles of Dorothy's life is that she remained part of a conflict-torn community for nearly half a century. Still more remarkable, she remained a person of hope and gratitude to the end. She occasionally spoke of "the duty of hope." Even in her final years, when hardly able to leave her room, she never ceased being a pilgrim.

Even though many have come to regard her as a saint, Dorothy was and remains a controversial woman. There was hardly anything she did that didn't attract criticism.

Even hospitality scandalizes some people. We were blamed for making people worse, not better, because we were doing nothing to "reform" them. A social worker once asked Dorothy how long the down-and-out were permitted to stay. "We let them stay forever," Dorothy answered brusquely. "They live with us, they die with us, and we give them a Christian burial. We pray for them after they are dead. Once they are taken in, they become members of the family. Or rather they always were members of the family. They are our brothers and sisters in Christ."

But what got her in the most hot water were her sharp social criticisms and her rejection of war. She pointed out that patriotism was a far more powerful force in the lives of most Christians than the gospel. While she hated every form of tyranny and never ceased to be thankful for America having taken in so many people fleeing poverty and repression, she was fierce in her criticism of capitalism and consumerism. She said America had a tendency to treat people like Kleenex—use them and throw them away. "Our problems stem," she once said, "from our acceptance of this filthy, rotten system."

She had no kind words for war or anything having to do with it—war was simply murder wrapped in flags. She was convinced Jesus had disarmed all his followers when he said to Peter, "Put your sword back into its place; for all who take the sword will perish by the sword" (Mt 26:52). A way of life based on love, including love of enemies, left no room for killing. We can't practice the works of mercy with one hand, she pointed out, and works of vengeance with the other.

No stranger to prison, Dorothy first went to jail as a young woman when she joined the Suffragettes in a protest in front of the White House during World War I. She was last jailed in her seventies for picketing with farm workers in California. She took pride in the young men of the Catholic Worker who went to prison rather than be drafted—"a good way to visit the prisoner," she pointed out. Yet she also welcomed back others who had left Catholic Worker communities to fight in the Second World War. They might disagree about the best way to fight Nazism, but—as she often said—"there is no 'party line' in the Catholic Worker movement."

Dorothy was sometimes criticized for being too orthodox in her religious convictions. How could she be so radical about social matters and so conservative in her theology? While she occasionally deplored statements or actions by members of the hierarchy, she was by no means an opponent of the bishops or someone furiously campaigning for structural changes in the church. What was needed, she said, wasn't new doctrine but living the existing doctrine. True, some pastors seemed barely Christian, but one had to aim for their conversion, an event that would not be hastened by berating them but rather by helping them see what their vocation required. The way to do that was to set an example.

Pleased as she was when the liturgy could be celebrated in English as well as Latin, she didn't take kindly to smudging the border between the sacred and mundane. When a radical priest used a coffee cup for a chalice at a Mass celebrated in the Catholic Worker house on First Street in Manhattan, she afterward took the cup, kissed it, and buried it in the back yard. It was no longer suited for coffee, she said, for it had held the Blood of Christ. I learned more about the Eucharist that day than I had from any book or sermon.

I'm sometimes told, "Dorothy Day gives a fine example for people who don't have a family to take care of and mortgages to pay, but what about the rest of us?"

The rest of us includes my wife and me. I don't have enough fingers on one hand to count our children, and I know all about paying a mortgage. But every time we open the door to guests, it is partly thanks to Dorothy Day. Every time I think about things in the bright light of the gospel rather than in the gray light of money or the dim light of politics, her example has had its influence. Every time I try to overcome meanness or selfishness rising up in myself, it is partly thanks to the example of Dorothy Day. Every time I defeat the impulse to buy something I can get along without, Dorothy Day's example of voluntary poverty has had renewed impact. Every time I try to see Christ's presence in the face of a stranger, there again I owe a debt to Dorothy Day. No one else has made me think so much about the words we will hear at the Last Judgment: "What you did to the least person, you did to me." What I know of Christ, the church, sacramental life, the Bible, and truth-telling, I know in large measure thanks to her, while whatever I have done that was cowardly, opportunistic, or cruel is despite her. She has even influenced my reading life—it was Dorothy who steered me to Dostoevsky's novels.

It isn't that Dorothy Day is the point of reference. Christ is. But I can't think of anyone I've known whose Christ-centered life did so much to help make me a more Christ-centered person.

It has been more than a century since Dorothy Day was born and more than a quarter-century since she died, but she continues to touch our lives, not only as a person we remember with gratitude but also as a saint—if by the word *saint* we mean a person who helps us see, by both precept and example, what it means to follow Christ.

"If I have accomplished anything in my life," she said late in her life, "it is because I wasn't embarrassed to talk about God."

The Road to Emmaus

You're not a pilgrim if you stay where you are.
                                                    —PAUL CHANDLER

*I believe my vocation is essentially that of a pilgrim and
an exile in life, that I have no proper place in the world,
but that for that reason I am in some sense to be the
friend and brother of people everywhere, especially those
who are exiles and pilgrims like myself. . . . My life is in
many ways simple, but it is also a mystery which I do
not attempt to really understand, as though I were led
by the hand in the night where I see nothing, but can
fully depend on the Love and Protection of Him who
guides me.*
                            —THOMAS MERTON, *COLD WAR LETTERS*

*When he was at table with them, he took the bread,
blessed and broke it, and gave it to them. Then their eyes
were opened, and they recognized him.*
                                                    —LUKE 24:30–31

Each of the stories about Christ's resurrection is a challenge to the rational part of ourselves. There is the account
in John's gospel of Mary Magdalene's encounter with him
near the empty tomb. Until he speaks to her by name, she
thinks he must be the gardener. Once she realizes who he is,
Jesus tells her not to touch him. Why? There are many
guesses, but in fact we don't know.

Though risen from the dead, he still bears the wounds that caused his death. Thomas, the apostle who was the most reluctant to make a leap of faith, becomes the only man to touch the wounds of the risen Christ. Why isn't Jesus fully healed? We don't know.

Soon after, on the shores of the Sea of Galilee, Jesus–a man freed from mortality–joins his friends in eating fish cooked over an open fire. Why is he who has become deathless still hungry? We don't know.

We know Christ rose from the dead and are familiar with the stories the gospel preserves for us of encounters people had with him before the ascension, but the mystery of his resurrection is beyond our intellectual reach.

Perhaps the most accessible of the resurrection narratives concerns the risen Christ's short pilgrimage with two disciples to Emmaus, a village described as being seven miles–less than a two-hour walk–from Jerusalem.

Two friends are escaping from a tragedy in Jerusalem and perhaps also running from personal danger. It wasn't at all clear that Jesus' disciples weren't next in line for punishment. The two were not only mourners, but disillusioned mourners. Jesus had failed to meet their expectations. The person they fervently believed would become the new king of Israel, heir to David's throne, not only wasn't ruling Israel but was in his grave. The candle of their messianic hopes has been snuffed out. His closest followers were in hiding. Their homeland was still ruled by Romans, undergirded by a second tier of well-rewarded Jewish collaborators. The kingdom of God that Jesus had said was already present now seemed infinitely distant.

Conversation would not have been easy. Deep grief rarely produces a talkative condition. The words they hewed out of silence were confused, bitter, angry. Their beloved teacher was dead and buried. Everything that mattered had turned to dust. The world had no center. Life's axis had crumbled.

Death once again had proven itself life's defining event. Existence had no meaning, no pattern. People of virtue perish while their persecutors feast. How could one speak of a merciful and all-powerful God? Ruthless power, corruption, betrayal, and the triumph of the grave—this was Good Friday's bitter message.

What person old enough to have attended a funeral of a deeply loved person whose life was cut short hasn't known a similar rage, numbness, and despair?

Walking side by side, breathing dust, the two friends are joined by a stranger who appears without a word of description. He doesn't impress the friends as being familiar. They fail to notice his wounds. Without apology he joins their conversation. He wonders why they are so downcast. They

The disciples at Emmaus by Rembrandt

are amazed at the stranger's ignorance. One of the disciples, Cleopas, asks the stranger how is it possible that he doesn't know what has happened in Jerusalem in recent days. Could anyone share in this particular Passover and be unaware of what had happened to Jesus of Nazareth? Only a week ago Jesus had entered the city in triumph, joyful crowds putting palms in his path and shouting hosannas. Then the man who should have redeemed Israel had been condemned by the high priests, renounced by the very crowds that had cheered him, and sentenced to public execution under the authority of Rome's agent, Pontius Pilate. Finally, he had been ritually murdered while soldiers threw dice for his clothing. Jesus' followers had dared to hope for a miracle even when Jesus was taken away to Golgotha—after all, he had raised Lazarus from death—but the man who had been able to bring others back to life proved powerless to save himself. Yes, the two friends had heard the wild tale told earlier in the day by a few grief-stricken women—angels, an empty tomb, Jesus alive again—but truly it was an unbelievable tale.

The stranger listened patiently. At last he responded, "Oh, how foolish you are, and how slow of heart to believe all that the prophets have declared! Was it not necessary that the Messiah should suffer these things and then enter into his glory?" (Lk 24:25–26). Then, starting with Moses and going on to all the prophets, he explained all the scriptural texts concerning the Messiah.

By this time they had reached the outskirts of Emmaus, apparently the place where the two friends planned to end their journey or at least spend the night. The stranger appeared to be going further, but they were so taken with his authoritative explanations of the prophecies of scripture that they appealed to him to join them for a meal in the local inn. "Stay with us," they said, "because it is almost evening and the day is now nearly over" (Lk 24:29).

Even when they sat down to eat, the stranger was still nameless and unrecognized, yet it was he who presided at the table, taking bread, blessing it, breaking it, and giving it to them. It is at this point in Luke's gospel that we get one of the most breathtaking sentences in the New Testament: "Then their eyes were opened, and they recognized him" (Lk 24:31).

Perhaps they recognized him because, at last, they noticed his wounds as he blessed and broke the bread.

In their moment of realization, Jesus "vanished from their sight." Perhaps he actually disappeared; as we have seen in other resurrection stories, the risen Christ doesn't seem subject to the laws of physics. Or perhaps he chose that moment to leave the table in order to continue his journey, but his departure was unseen because the two disciples, weeping with joy, were momentarily blinded by their tears. We don't know. All we are sure of is that the stranger was Jesus and that the two disciples finally knew with whom they had been talking on their way to Emmaus, and who it was that blessed the bread and broke it.

They said to each other, "Were not our hearts burning within us while he was talking to us on the road, while he was opening the scriptures to us?" (Lk 24:32).

Forgetting their exhaustion and hunger, the two disciples reversed their journey, hurrying back to Jerusalem in order to report what they had witnessed. But by now, they discovered, it wasn't only the women who had proclaimed the resurrection. "The Lord has risen indeed," they were told, "and he has appeared to Simon!" (Lk 24:34).

What happened on the road to Emmaus, and finally in Emmaus itself, was the first Christian pilgrimage. Every pilgrimage, whether to a local park or to some distant place at the end of a well-trodden pilgrim road thick with miracles, is in its roots a journey to Emmaus, and every pilgrimage is animated with a similar hope: to meet the risen Christ along the way.

It is a hope one hardly dares to mention. Yet something like the Emmaus story occurs in many lives. Again and again we meet strangers along the way who speak with unexpected clarity about things that really matter. In such encounters, do we not find our hearts aflame within us? This is a person we are in no hurry to part from, whose words and presence are water in the desert. The stranger is someone whom we would eagerly invite to eat with us even if we had little money to spare, someone with whom we are eager to break bread.

At the heart of the Emmaus story is the stranger. Had the two disciples failed to make room for him in their journey, the New Testament would be missing one of its most illuminating stories.

Pilgrimage is not possible if it excludes unexpected people found along the way. Perhaps it is only for an hour or a day. A hesitant conversation takes wing. A reluctant tongue becomes fluent. Finally, we eat together. By now, the stranger has become a named person—José, Carl, or Ahmed, Maria, Larissa, or Teresa. Sooner or later we part, but we remember that encounter as a shining moment. We didn't literally meet Jesus risen from the dead, and yet, in this brief communion with a stranger, Jesus became present and traveled with us. A chance encounter became a eucharistic event. Ideas about Jesus were replaced with an experience of Jesus.

The details of such encounters vary infinitely. No two God-revealing encounters are the same. Each of us is unique, and each of us experiences conversion in unique ways, even though we recognize something of our own conversion in all the conversion stories we happen to hear. *Conversion* means "a deep turning." Each of the conversions I experience shifts the way I see, hear, and act. Each conversion is a freeing event. Something I desperately and addictively needed yesterday has become superfluous today. Certain fears I previously struggled with have been burned away.

There is not one conversion in life. Conversion follows conversion like an ascending ladder. Each rung reveals another. It is a slow process, one that can never be forced or hurried. We are still busy being converted when we die. A good title for any autobiography would be the three-word message a computer occasionally displays when changing a file from one program format to another: *Conversion in progress.*

Conversion isn't something we do entirely on our own. As pilgrims, the main challenge is not to miss Jesus along the way. It requires the recognition that, no matter how alone we are, there are no solitary journeys. Life is a series of meetings. The only question is how deep we allow the meetings to be. The "I" exists only in communion with others.

We interact with other people every day: family members, friends, neighbors, co-workers, plus many people we don't know by name, people we meet briefly in shops, on buses, on trains, behind counters, beggars on the street. Whether known by name or an anonymous stranger, how much real contact occurs is partly up to us. Even people living or working under the same roof can be too busy, too irritated, or too fearful for real contact to occur.

But there is always the possibility of conversation that moves beyond the exchange of distance-keeping civilities. To be a pilgrim—to be on the road to Emmaus—is to be open to contact, willing to share stories, willing to talk about the real issues in one's life, willing to listen with undivided attention.

"Our life and our death is with our neighbor," said Saint Anthony the Great, founder of Christian monasticism. "If we win our brother, we win God. If we cause our brother to stumble, we have sinned against Christ."[53]

There is no such thing as finding Christ while avoiding our neighbor. The main thing impeding that encounter is our suffocating fear of the other. As the Orthodox theologian Metropolitan John Zizioulas comments:

Communion with the other is not spontaneous; it is built upon fences which protect us from the dangers implicit in the other's presence. We accept the other only insofar as he does not threaten our privacy or insofar as he is useful to our individual happiness. . . . The essence of sin is the fear of the Other, which is part of the rejection of God. Once the affirmation of the "self" is realized through the rejection and not the acceptance of the Other–this is what Adam chose in his freedom to do–it is only natural and inevitable for the other to become an enemy and a threat. Reconciliation with God is a necessary pre-condition for reconciliation with any "other."[54]

That last sentence also works in reverse: Reconciliation with the other is a necessary precondition for reconciliation with God. As Saint John writes, "Whoever says, 'I am in the light,' while hating a brother or sister, is still in the darkness" (1 Jn 2:9). The path to heaven leads through the rush-hour traffic of the human race.

At the heart of pilgrimage is the struggle not to let our dread of the other prevent meetings with strangers. Just as on the road to Emmaus, it is in the disguise of the stranger that Christ appears.

I often think of a nun who gave me a ride from Louisville to Lexington when I was in Kentucky to give a few lectures. It is now too long ago for me to remember her name, but I will never forget the spirit of welcome that she radiated. Her old, battered car is also not easily forgotten, though it would have been worth little in a used-car lot. In her care it had become a house of hospitality on wheels. As we drove along the highway, the glove-compartment door in front of me kept popping open. I closed it repeatedly, each time noticing a pile of maps inside and also a book. At last the text on the spine of the book caught my eye: *Guests*. I pulled it out, discovering page after page of signatures, most of which gave the impression that the person signing was barely literate.

"What is this?" I asked.

"Oh, that's my guest book."

"But why keep it in the car?"

"Well, of course, I always pick up hitchhikers, so I need a guest book."

I was astonished. Picking up hitchhikers was not without risks, especially for women.

"But isn't that dangerous?" I asked.

"Well, I have had many guests sitting where you are now, most of them men, and I never felt I was in danger."

She went on to explain that when she pulled over to offer a ride, she immediately introduced herself by name. Then she asked, "And what is your name?"

The immediate exchange of names, she explained, was a crucial first step in hospitality and one likely to make for safety.

"Once two people entrust their names to each other," she explained, "there is a personal relationship."

The next step was to ask the guest to put his name in writing: "I would be grateful if you would sign my guest book."

She didn't have to explain to me that few of the people she had given rides to had ever been regarded as anyone's guests, and fewer still had been invited to sign a guest book.

"I've met many fine people," she told me, "people who have been a blessing to me. I never had any troubles, though you could see that many of them had lived a hard life."

Before saying goodbye, she had me sign her guest book.

Anyone reading the lives of the saints will notice that life-changing meetings with strangers are not rare events. Martin of Tours, one of the major saints of the fourth century, had one such encounter not long before his baptism. A detailed retelling of the story is included in *Butler's Lives of the Saints:*

One day, in the midst of a very hard winter and severe frost, when many perished with cold, as Martin was marching with other officers and soldiers, he met at the gate of the city of Amiens a poor man, almost naked, trembling and shaking with cold, and begging alms of those that passed by. Martin, seeing those that went before him take no notice of this miserable object, thought he was reserved for himself. By his charities to others he had nothing left but his arms and clothes upon his back; when, drawing his sword, he cut his cloak in two pieces, gave one to the beggar, and wrapped himself in the other half. Some of the bystanders laughed at the figure he made in that dress, whilst others were ashamed not to have relieved the poor man. In the following night St. Martin saw in his sleep Jesus Christ dressed in that half of the garment which he had given away, and was bid to look at it well and asked whether he knew it. He then heard Jesus say, "Martin, yet a catechumen, has clothed me with this garment." This vision inspired the saint with fresh ardor, and determined him speedily to receive baptism, which he did in the eighteenth year of his age.[55]

One extravagant act led to another. Two years after his baptism, Martin—still in the army—risked his life by refusing to take part in battle. "I am a soldier of Christ," he explained on the eve of battle. "It is not lawful for me to fight." Accused of being a coward, Martin volunteered to stand unarmed before the enemy. Miraculously, the enemy sued for peace. Caesar afterward allowed Martin to resign his army commission. Martin went on to become one of the most distinguished missionary bishops of the early church. He who converted many owed his own conversion to an encounter with a nameless beggar in Amiens.

It is a never-ending story. Whatever real growth I may attain in my life is chiefly thanks to the care and love, the welcome and hospitality, provided by others who see in me qualities I cannot see, who somehow assist me in deepening my faith, who open a window revealing the risen Christ. Often the unexpected encounters come not from people who are obliged by family ties to care for me, but from strangers met along my particular pilgrim path. Indeed it is often thanks to strangers that we discover that we are on pilgrimage.

Pick any century, pick just about any saint, dig carefully enough into the stories that have come down to us, and again and again one finds both pilgrim and stranger.

As the life of grace deepens, many saints are no longer willing to wait to meet strangers by chance, but make it their business to do the finding.

Among recent examples of those who each day sought Christ in the poor are Mother Teresa and Dorothy Day. "I see God in every human being," Mother Teresa often said. "When I wash the leper's wounds, I feel I am nursing the Lord himself. Is it not a beautiful experience?"

"Those who cannot see Christ in the poor," said Dorothy Day, "are atheists indeed."

Another saint of the same generation is Mother Maria Skobtsova, a recently canonized Orthodox nun. Like Dorothy Day, she founded a house of hospitality. Indeed, in both women's lives it happened in the same year, 1933, one in New York, the other in Paris.

In 1940, when the German army marched into Paris, hospitality became a vocation involving huge risks. Taking in many Jews and finding places of safety for them, Mother Maria and her co-workers were well aware they were courting arrest. In the end, she and three others from the same community died in Nazi concentration camps.

At the heart of Mother Maria's countless acts of welcoming strangers was her conviction that each person without exception bears the image of God. She wrote:

If someone turns with his spiritual world toward the spiritual world of another person, he encounters an awesome and inspiring mystery. He comes into contact with the true image of God in man, with the very icon of God incarnate in the world, with a reflection of the mystery of God's incarnation and divine manhood. And he needs to accept this awesome revelation of God unconditionally, to venerate the image of God in his brother. Only when he senses, perceives and understands it will yet another mystery be revealed to him—one that will demand his most dedicated efforts. He will perceive that the divine image is veiled, distorted and disfigured by the power of evil. And he will want to engage in battle with the devil for the sake of the divine image.[56]

The Russian writer Aleksandr Solzhenitsyn made the same discovery, in his case while a prisoner in Stalin's archipelago of concentration camps, an environment of profound contempt for life. While witnessing cruelty day after day, Solzhenitsyn found the anger and hatred that he felt gradually being replaced by compassion. As religious faith took the place of Marxist ideology, it became more and more evident to him that no human being has ever been born in whom there is no trace of the Creator. Even the most vile person at certain moments reveals some evidence of God. As he wrote in *The Gulag Archipelago:*

The line separating good and evil passes not through states, nor between classes, nor between political parties either—but right through every human heart—and through all human hearts. This line shifts. Inside us, it oscillates with the years. And even within hearts overwhelmed by evil, one small bridgehead of good is retained. And even in the best of hearts, there remains . . . an un-uprooted small corner of evil.[57]

Mainly one learns this only in the crucible of life. It is a truth rarely revealed in movies. In films those who *do* evil tend to *be* evil. The evil is imbedded in their DNA. They had a pathological twist before they were born. The only cure for such pure evil is death. Thus killing evil people is an act of a virtue. It is what heroes do. Far from wanting to meet such people and search in them for a "small bridgehead of good," we either applaud their execution or, should our awareness of the mercy of Christ protect us from advocating killing as a solution, insist that they be locked up as long and grimly as possible, ideally until claimed by the grave. Seeing how merciless such people have been, we are tempted to think that they deserve no mercy and can never change for the better. In fact, we behave toward them in a way that makes our dire expectations all the more likely.

A great problem of thinking along such grim, vindictive lines—imagining we know a person we know only through clippings or movies and resolutely refusing to search for God's image in that person—is that we exclude ourselves from walking on the road to Emmaus.

But being a pilgrim is not a naive undertaking. There are, we know, strangers who are dangerous. Should our fear of violence lead us to avoid all strangers for that reason? Should our fear of death lead us to live cautiously?

Christian pilgrims have always known that they might die on the way, like countless thousands of pilgrims before them. Statistically, unexpected death along the way may be less likely for the modern pilgrim than it was in earlier times, but still accidents happen, grave sicknesses occur, and there are occasional acts of violence and even murder.

The pilgrim's attitude traditionally has been: "Sooner or later I die. If it happens while on pilgrimage, what better way to cross life's final border? Why be afraid?"

Pilgrimage is not getting from point A to point B on the map while counting the miles. The distances covered are

incidental. What matters is being on the road to Emmaus–
the road of discovering Christ in the "other."

Pilgrimage was, and still is, the great adventure of shedding the scales of blindness. We discover it is impossible not
to be in the presence of God. God is with us all the time, of
course, only we don't notice. It is not that we are technically
blind. We may be able to read the small print in an insur-
ance contract without glasses and to make out the shape of a
high-flying jet, and yet there is so much we don't yet see that
we live in a darkness that is not unlike actual blindness. It is
a condition not caused by physical damage but by deeply
rooted fears, the imprisonment of self-absorption, and ideological obsessions.

Walking the road to Emmaus, as a Christian on permanent pilgrimage, is the great journey into real seeing. In words
ascribed to Saint Patrick:

> *Christ with me, Christ before me, Christ behind me,*
> *Christ in me, Christ beneath me, Christ above me,*
> *Christ on my right, Christ on my left,*
> *Christ when I lie down, Christ when I sit down,*
>   *Christ when I arise, Christ in the heart of*
>   *everyone who thinks of me,*
> *Christ in the mouth of every one who speaks of me,*
> *Christ in every eye that sees me,*
> *Christ in every ear that hears me.*

A Prayer for Pilgrims

Lord Jesus, you traveled with the two disciples to
Emmaus after the resurrection and set their
hearts on fire with your grace. Travel also with
me and gladden my heart with your presence.
I know, Lord, that I am a pilgrim on earth,
seeking citizenship in heaven.
During my journey surround me with your holy
angels and keep me safe from seen and unseen
dangers.
Grant that I may carry out my plans and fulfill my
expectations according to your will.
Help me to see the beauty of creation and to
comprehend the wonder of your truth in all
things.
For you are the way, the truth, and the life, and to
you I give thanks, praise, and glory forever.
Amen.

Appreciation

$\mathcal{I}$ cannot imagine what would be between the covers of this book if it weren't for my wife, Nancy. Not only are some of the stories related here stolen from her, but much of the structure of the book has grown out of countless conversations, some while traveling, others over the table.

Then there has been the role of Robert Ellsberg, my friend of many years and in recent decades my editor as well. I cherish the memory of a day three decades ago when we went together as pilgrims to Chartres. I cannot imagine a better friend or editor.

Dorothy Day has had a hand in this, even though it has been many years since she died. She is my model pilgrim.

Thomas Merton helped me understand how confined the geography of one's life can be and yet how each day can be an act of pilgrimage.

Henri Nouwen, another friend who has slipped across life's final border, taught me about the long pilgrimage it is just to find one's vocation.

Thich Nhat Hanh taught me a lot about two of life's simplest skills, breathing and walking, without which no pilgrimage gets very far.

John Brady, fiddle player and man of deep thoughts, has read most if not all the chapters in this book in draft and given me a great deal of helpful advice.

The same is true for Sally Eckert and Piet Dykstra. Whatever mistakes in grammar you may discover in this book are there only because I don't always follow their guidance.

Last but not least, my gratitude goes to my most conscientious copy editor, Joan Weber Laflamme.

Notes

1. Hillaire Belloc, *The Old Road* (London: Constable, 1904).

2. Shirley du Boulay, *The Road to Canterbury: A Modern Pilgrimage* (London: Morehouse Group, 1995).

3. J. R. R. Tolkien, *The Fellowship of the Ring*, Book 1 of *The Lord of the Rings* (New York: Ballantine Books, 1965), 62.

4. Dorothy Day, *The Long Loneliness* (New York: Harper, 1952), 37.

5. Ibid., 38.

6. I was in prison for a year in 1969–70 for having been one of the Milwaukee Fourteen, a group that burned draft records as an act of resistance to the Vietnam War. For details, see http://incommunion .org/forest-flier/jimsessays/looking-back-on-the-milwaukee-14/.

7. Benedicta Ward, *In Company with Christ* (London: SPCK, 2005).

8. Abbot Christopher Jamison, *Finding Sanctuary: Monastic Steps for Everyday Life* (London: Weidenfeld and Nicolson, 2006), 53.

9. One of the best Orthodox introductions to prayer, with extensive extracts from letters of guidance by Saint Theofan the Recluse, is *The Art of Prayer*, ed. Igumen Chariton (London: Faber and Faber, 1936). On the descent of the mind into the heart, see pages 22, 183–84, 185–86, and 189.

10. For more on this topic, see Jim Forest, *Praying with Icons* (Maryknoll, NY: Orbis Books, 1998).

11. *The Way of the Pilgrim*, translated by R. M. French, was first published in English in 1930. The original Russian edition (with the title that translates as *The Candid Narratives of a Pilgrim to His Spiritual Father*) was published in 1884, having been copied from a manuscript a Russian abbot discovered during a stay at one of the monasteries on Mount Athos. The book appears to have been written shortly before the liberation of the serfs in 1861. The name of the author has never been discovered. There is a continuation of the book entitled *The Pilgrim Continues His Way*. Some editions combine both volumes. *The Way of the Pilgrim* has helped create an interest in *The Philokalia*. Four volumes now exist in English translation with a fifth and final volume in preparation. Also of great value is *The Art of Prayer,* compiled by Igumen Chariton of Valamo; *The Jesus Prayer* by "A Monk of the

Eastern Church" [Fr. Lev Gillet]; and *The Power of the Name* by Bishop Kallistos of Diokleia.

12. Boris Vysheslavtsev, cited in J. P. Dunlop, *Staretz Amvrosy* (Belmont, MA: BVA Books, 1972), 22.

13. Henri Nouwen, *Clowning in Rome* (New York: Image Books, 1979), 70.

14. Bob Lax, letter to *Jubilee* magazine staff, quoted in Jim Harford, *Merton and Friends* (New York: Continuum, 2006), 105–6.

15. Benedicta Ward, ed., *The Sayings of the Desert Fathers: The Alphabetical Collection*, Cistercian Studies 59 (Kalamazoo, MI: Cistercian Publications, 1984), 81.

16. Ignatius of Antioch, "Chapter XV–Exhortation to Confess Christ by Silence as Well as Speech." See the online collection of writings of the apostolic fathers on the ccel.org website.

17. John Climacus, *The Ladder of Divine Ascent*, "Step 11: On Talkativeness and Silence" (Mahwah, NJ: Paulist Press, 1982), 158.

18. Ranier Maria Rilke, *Letters to a Young Poet*, trans. Stephen Mitchell (New York: Modern Library, 2001), 4.

19. Thomas Merton, *The Hidden Ground of Love: The Letters of Thomas Merton on Religious Experience and Social Concerns*, ed. William H. Shannon (New York: Farrar, Straus, Giroux, 1985), 473–74. See also the chapter entitled "Merton and the Christ of the Byzantine Icons" in Jim Forest, *Living with Wisdom: A Life of Thomas Merton* (Maryknoll, NY: Orbis Books, 1991).

20. It is only recently that I learned the story of Saint Nikita (sometimes rendered Nicetas) of Novgorod, thanks to John Brady's website on the saints of the Orthodox church. Here is a shortened version. Nikita was a young and zealous monk who belonged to the monastic community living in the caves of Kiev. Against the advice of his abbot, Saint Nikon, he decided to embrace a more extreme ascetic life, walling himself into a cave. Some time later, he experienced a delightful scent filling his enclosure. Believing himself to be receiving a divine revelation, he cried out, "Lord, show yourself to me, that I might worship you face to face!" A voice–it turned out to be from a demon–answered, "I am sending you an angel: do whatever he tells you." The demon soon appeared to him disguised as an angel of light. Completely taken in, Nikita prostrated himself before the apparition. The demon ordered him to stop praying and instead to devote all his time to reading and memorizing the Old Testament. Nikita obeyed without question. After a while the devil began to reveal to him things that were happening in the outside world, so that, among visitors to his cave, Nikita acquired a reputation for prophecy. When his monastic elders realized that Nikita never spoke to anyone about the

New Testament, they realized he had been beguiled by a demon. As a result they forced him to leave his hermit's enclosure, drove the demon away by their prayers, and brought the young monk back to community life. Once the demon had been driven off, Nikita became like a child. Not only did he forget all that he had memorized, but he even lost his ability to read, so that he had to be sent to school again. Slowly he returned to himself, realized his former delusion, and repented in tears, devoting himself to humility and obedience in the community. Such was his repentance and progress in the virtues that he was later made bishop of Novgorod. His life in this world ended in 1108. He became known for many miracles, especially the healing of blindness. (See the entry for January 31 at www.abbamoses.com/months/january.html.)

21. For a more detailed biography of Saint Matrona, see Brenda Meehan, *Holy Women of Russia* (San Francisco: HarperSanFrancisco, 1993), 61–78.

22. Saint Alexis, the only son of a wealthy Roman senator, was taught by his parents to be charitable to the poor. Alexis wanted to give up his wealth and honors, but his parents had chosen a rich bride for him. Because it was their will, he married her. Yet, on his wedding day, he obtained his wife's permission to leave her for God. In disguise, he traveled to Syria and lived in great poverty near a church of Our Lady. Praying before an icon of Christ's mother, he heard her voice describing him as a holy beggar. He returned to Rome and assumed the life of begging, sharing what was given to him with others living on the streets. His parents did not recognize him, but they were kind to all poor people and so they let him stay in a corner beneath the stairs. There Alexis is said to have spent his nights for seventeen years. He used to go out only to pray in church and to teach little children about God. The servants were often cruel to him. After Alexis died in 417 his family found a note on his body that told them who he was and explained the beggar vocation to which God had called him.

23. Orthodox Christians may attend Orthros and liturgy within the monastery if they present themselves at the gate at 5 a.m.

24. Most pilgrims these days take the camel trail, which is broader, less steep, and with many more switchbacks.

25. A good starting point is Thomas Merton's *The Wisdom of the Desert.* There is also Helen Waddell's classic study *The Desert Fathers.* Benedicta Ward has brought out a wonderful series of texts, among them *The Sayings of the Desert Fathers: The Alphabetical Collection; The Lives of the Desert Fathers; The Wisdom of the Desert Fathers;* and *Harlots of the Desert.* A Benedictine nun, Laura Swan, has recently published *The Forgotten Desert Mothers.*

26. For a detailed history of the church plus a great many photos, see the Franciscan website at http://www.christusrex.org/www1/ofm/TSspmain.html.

27. Today the abbey is home to the Iona Community, which describes itself as "an ecumenical Christian community of men and women from different walks of life and different traditions in the Christian church that is committed to seeking new ways of living the gospel of Jesus Christ in today's world" (see the community's website at http://www.iona.org.uk/).

28. See http://www.annefrank.org.

29. See http://www.dorothydaymemphis.org/.

30. See http://americanradioworks.publicradio.org/features/sayitplain/mlking.html.

31. By 1861 Memphis was of two minds about the impending war. The cotton trade tied Memphis to Northern industry to such an extent that many did not want to secede from the Union. On the other hand, plantation owners were dependent on slave labor. Loyalties were split not only between neighbors but within families.

32. It is estimated that at its height, between 1810 and 1850, between 30,000 and 100,000 people escaped enslavement by way of the Underground Railroad.

33. For more on religious life in Albania, see Jim Forest, *The Resurrection of the Church in Albania* (Geneva: World Council of Churches, 2002).

34. Thomas Merton, *Conjectures of a Guilty Bystander* (New York: Doubleday, 1966), 140–42.

35. Thomas Merton, "Preface," *The Seven Storey Mountain,* Japanese edition (1966); also published in *Introductions East and West: The Foreign Prefaces of Thomas Merton,* ed. Robert E. Daggy (Greensboro, NC: Unicorn Press, 1981) and *Honorable Reader: Reflections on My Work,* ed. Robert E. Daggy (New York: Crossroad, 1989).

36. Nancy Forest, "Right Where I'm Standing," in *Toward the Authentic Church: Orthodox Discuss Their Conversion,* ed. Thomas Doulis (Minneapolis, MN: Light and Life Books, 1996). Also available on the incommunion.org website.

37. Thomas Merton, *New Seeds of Contemplation* (New York: New Directions, 1961), 112. Also available at http://tcrnews2.com/peace2.html. For a section of text that was not included with the essay in the book version, see Forest, *Living with Wisdom,* 135–38.

38. "Use of Anti-Anxiety Drugs Jumps in U.S.: Number of New Prescriptions Increases Sharply in Washington and New York," report by Susan Okie, *The Washington Post,* October 14, 2001. It should be noted that the use of antidepressants was already high before 9/11.

The percentage of adults using antidepressants almost tripled between 1988–94 and 1999–2000 ("Health, United States, 2004: With Chartbook on Trends in the Health of Americans," a report published by the National Center for Health Statistics of the US Department of Health and Social Services Centers for Disease Control and Prevention [2004]).

39. President George W. Bush, speech, Cincinnati, Ohio, October 7, 2002.

40. Psychiatrist Clotaire Rapaille, a consultant to the automobile industry, conducted studies of Iraq War psychological consumer profiles for the Chrysler Corporation. He reported that Americans wanted "aggressive" cars. SUVs, Rapaille said, were being sold as "armored cars for the battlefield," thus appealing to buyers' fears of violence (*The Guardian,* July 12, 2003). Another hostility-intensification feature is the "grill guard" promoted by SUV manufacturers. Grill guards, useful mainly for nudging cattle off the road, have no application under normal driving conditions, but they make SUVs look more threatening when viewed through a rearview mirror. They also increase the chance that an SUV will kill someone in an accident. Deliberately marketed as "urban assault luxury vehicles," far from making their owners safer, they increase the danger to both driver and passengers. Due to SUVs' propensity for rollovers, the occupant death rate in SUVs is six to eight percent higher than in ordinary cars. They also get worse mileage. Hummers average a mere eight to ten miles a gallon, a figure that takes on additional significance in light of the role that dependency on foreign oil has played in shaping US relations with countries in the Middle East.

41. The Saint George portion of the *Legenda Aurea* is available at http://www.fordham.edu/halsall/basis/goldenlegend/GL-vol3-george.html.

42. Fr. Alexander Schmemann, "On the Nativity of the Mother of God," in *Celebration of Faith,* vol. 3, *The Virgin Mary,* trans. Fr. John Jillions (Crestwood, NY: St. Vladimir's Seminary Press, 1995), 24.

43. See http://www.dorothydaymemphis.org/.

44. Nancy Louise Frey, *Pilgrim Stories: On and Off the Road to Santiago* (Berkeley and Los Angeles: University of California Press, 1998), 73.

45. Abel Herzberg, *Brieven aan mijn kleinzoon* [Letters to My Grandson] (Amsterdam: Querido, 1985), 126. Translation by Nancy Forest.

46. Dorothy Day, "On Pilgrimage," *The Catholic Worker* (December 1965); also see the Dorothy Day Web Library, Document #248 at http://www.catholicworker.org/dorothyday/daytext.cfm?TextID=248.

47. For extensive extracts from Dorothy Day's writing on Saint Thérèse of Lisieux, see Robert Ellsberg, ed., *Dorothy Day: Selected Writings* (Maryknoll, NY: Orbis Books, 2005), 187–203.

48. *The Letters of William James,* ed. by his son Henry James (Boston: Atlantic Monthy Press, 1920), 2:90; letter to Mrs. Henry Whitman, June 7, 1899.

49. Bettina Selby, *Pilgrim's Road: A Journey to Santiago de Compostela* (London: Little, Brown, 1994), 211–12.

50. Frey, *Pilgrim Stories,* 84–85.

51. Tatiana Goricheva, *Talking about God Is Dangerous* (New York: Crossroad, 1987), 70.

52. Robert Coles, *Dorothy Day: A Radical Devotion* (Reading, MA: Addison-Wesley, 1987).

53. Benedicta Ward, *The Sayings of the Desert Fathers: The Alphabetical Collection,* Cistercian Studies 59 (Kalamazoo, MI: Cistercian Publications, 1984), see Anthony 9.

54. John Zizioulas, "Communion and Otherness," Orthodox Peace Fellowship Occasional Paper no. 19 (Summer 1994). Available at http://incommunion.org/articles/previous-issues/older-issues/communion-and-otherness.

55. Herbert Thornton and Donald Attwater, eds., *Butler's Lives of the Saints,* 4 vols. (1963). Note that *Butler's Lives of the Saints* was first published in the eighteenth century and has been repeatedly revised in later years. The entry about Saint Martin is available at http://www.ewtn.com/library/mary/stmartin.htm.

56. Mother Maria Skobtsova, "The Second Gospel Commandment" in *Mother Maria Skobtsova: Essential Writings,* ed. Hélène Arjakovsky-Klépinine, trans. Richard Pevear and Larissa Volokhonsky (Maryknoll, NY: Orbis Books, 2003). For more information on Mother Maria Skobtsova, see Fr. Sergei Hackel, *Pearl of Great Price: A Biography of Mother Maria Skobtsova* (Crestwood, NY: St. Vladimir's Seminary Press, 1981); T. Stratton Smith, *The Rebel Nun* (Springfield, IL: Templegate, 1965); Jim Forest, *Silent as a Stone: Mother Maria of Paris and the Trash Can Rescue* (Crestwood, NY: St. Vladimir's Seminary Press, 2007). For other resources, see the Mother Maria section of the incommunion.org website.

57. Aleksandr Solzhenitsyn, *The Gulag Archipelago 1918–1956: An Experiment in Literary Investigation 1–II,* vol. 2, *The Ascent,* trans. Thomas P. Whitney (Harper Collins, 1974).